How To Use This Study Guide

This ten-lesson study guide corresponds to *"How To Float on a Sea of Destruction in the Last Days" With Rick Renner* (**Renner TV**). Each lesson in this study guide covers a topic that is addressed during the program series, with questions and references supplied to draw you deeper into your own private study of the Scriptures on this subject.

To derive the most benefit from this study guide, consider the following:

First, watch or listen to the program prior to working through the corresponding lesson in this guide. (Programs can also be viewed at **renner.org** by clicking on the Media/Archives links or on our Renner Ministries YouTube channel.)

Second, take the time to look up the scriptures included in each lesson. Prayerfully consider their application to your own life.

Third, use a journal or notebook to make note of your answers to each lesson's Study Questions and Practical Application challenges.

Fourth, invest specific time in prayer and in the Word of God to consult with the Holy Spirit. Write down the scriptures or insights He reveals to you.

Finally, take action! Whatever the Lord tells you to do according to His Word, do it.

For added insights on this subject, it is recommended that you obtain Rick Renner's book *Last-Days Survival Guide: A Scriptural Handbook To Prepare You for These Perilous Times*. You may also select from Rick's other available resources by placing your order at **renner.org** or by calling 1-800-742-5593.

LESSON 1

TOPIC
Are You Sealed Tight and Safe?

SCRIPTURES
1. **Matthew 24:37** — But as the days of Noe [Noah] were, so shall also the coming of the Son of man be.
2. **Genesis 7:16,17** — And they that went in, went in male and female of all flesh, as God had commanded him: and the Lord shut him in. And the flood was forty days upon the earth; and the waters increased, and bare up the ark, and it was lift up above the earth.
3. **Genesis 6:16** — A window shalt thou make to the ark, and in a cubit shalt thou finish it above; and the door of the ark shalt thou set in the side thereof; with lower, second, and third stories shalt thou make it.
4. **John 14:6** — Jesus saith unto him, I am the way, the truth, and the life: no man cometh unto the Father, but by me.
5. **Romans 10:8-13** — But what saith it? The word is nigh thee, even in thy mouth, and in thy heart: that is, the word of faith, which we preach; That if thou shalt confess with thy mouth the Lord Jesus, and shalt believe in thine heart that God hath raised him from the dead, thou shalt be saved. For with the heart man believeth unto righteousness; and with the mouth confession is made unto salvation. For the scripture saith, Whosoever believeth on him shall not be ashamed. For there is no difference between the Jew and the Greek: for the same Lord over all is rich unto all that call upon him. For whosoever shall call upon the name of the Lord shall be saved.
6. **1 Corinthians 12:13** — For by one Spirit are we all baptized into one body....
7. **Ephesians 1:1,3,4** — Paul, an apostle of Jesus Christ by the will of God, to the saints which are at Ephesus, and to the faithful in Christ Jesus:... Blessed be the God and Father of our Lord Jesus Christ, who hath blessed us with all spiritual blessings in heavenly places in Christ: According as he hath chosen us in him before the foundation of the world, that we should be holy and without blame before him in love.

A Note From Rick Renner

I am on a personal quest to see a "revival of the Bible" so people can establish their lives on a firm foundation that will stand strong and endure the test as end-time storm winds begin to intensify.

In order to experience a revival of the Bible in your personal life, it is important to take time each day to read, receive, and apply its truths to your life. James tells us that if we will continue in the perfect law of liberty — refusing to be forgetful hearers, but determined to be doers — we will be blessed in our ways. As you watch or listen to the programs in this series and work through this corresponding study guide, I trust you will search the Scriptures and allow the Holy Spirit to help you hear something new from God's Word that applies specifically to your life. I encourage you to be a doer of the Word He reveals to you. Whatever the cost, I assure you — it will be worth it.

> Thy words were found, and I did eat them;
> and thy word was unto me the joy and rejoicing of mine heart:
> for I am called by thy name, O Lord God of hosts.
> — Jeremiah 15:16

Your brother and friend in Jesus Christ,

Rick Renner

Unless otherwise indicated, all scripture quotations are taken from the *King James Version* of the Bible.

Scripture quotations marked (*AMPC*) are taken from the *Amplified® Bible, Classic Edition*. Copyright © 1954, 1958, 1962, 1964, 1965, 1987 by The Lockman Foundation. Used by permission. **www.Lockman.org**.

Scripture quotations marked (*CEV*) are from the *Contemporary English Version* Copyright © 1991, 1992, 1995 by American Bible Society. Used by Permission.

Scriptures marked as (*GNT*) are taken from the **Good News Translation - Second Edition** © 1992 by American Bible Society. Used by permission.

Scripture quotations marked (*NIV*) are taken from the *Holy Bible, New International Version®, NIV®* Copyright ©1973, 1978, 1984, 2011 by Biblica, Inc.® Used by permission. All rights reserved worldwide.

Scripture quotations marked (*NKJV*) are taken from the *New King James Version®*. Copyright © 1982 by Thomas Nelson. Used by permission. All rights reserved.

Scripture quotations marked (*NLT*) are taken from the Holy Bible, *New Living Translation*, copyright © 1996, 2004, 2015 by Tyndale House Foundation. Used by permission of Tyndale House Publishers, Inc., Carol Stream, Illinois 60188. All rights reserved.

Scripture quotations marked (*RIV*) are taken from *Renner Interpretive Version*. Copyright © 2021 by Rick Renner.

How To Float on a Sea of Destruction in the Last Days
10 Principles To Help You Sail Victoriously Through Turbulent End-Time Weather

Copyright © 2024 by Rick Renner
1814 W. Tacoma St.
Broken Arrow, OK 74012-1406

Published by Rick Renner Ministries
www.renner.org

ISBN 13: 978-1-6675-0638-8

ISBN 13 eBook: 978-1-6675-0639-5

All rights reserved. No portion of this book may be reproduced or transmitted in any form or by any means — electronic, mechanical, photocopy, recording, scanning, or other — except for brief quotations in critical reviews or articles, without the prior written permission of the Publisher.

8. **Ephesians 1:6,7** — To the praise of the glory of his grace, wherein he hath made us accepted in the beloved. In whom we have redemption through his blood, the forgiveness of sins, according to the riches of his grace.
9. **Ephesians 1:11** — In whom also we have obtained an inheritance, being predestinated according to the purpose of him who worketh all things after the counsel of his own will.
10. **Ephesians 1:13,14** — In whom ye also trusted, after that ye heard the word of truth, the gospel of your salvation: in whom also after that ye believed, ye were sealed with that holy Spirit of promise, which is the earnest of our inheritance until the redemption of the purchased possession, unto the praise of his glory.

GREEK WORDS

1. "salvation" — σωτηρία (*soteria*): expresses the ideas of present deliverance, healing, preservation, prosperity, safety, and general welfare
2. "sealed" — σφραγίζω (*sphragidzo*): pictures a seal placed on a package after the product had been thoroughly examined and inspected to make sure it was fully intact and complete; the seal was proof the product was impeccable; normally such seals bore the insignia of a wealthy or famous person, which meant that this package was to be treated with tender care; the seal affirmed who was the owner and guaranteed the package had sufficient postage paid to make it to its final destination
3. "earnest" — ἀρραβών (*arrabon*): a payment given in advance to guarantee the whole amount will be paid afterward; earnest money; an installment; a deposit; a down payment which guarantees full delivery of a promise; a security deposit given by the purchaser to assure confidence and peace to the seller that he will fulfill his promise

SYNOPSIS

The ten lessons in this study on ***How To Float on a Sea of Destruction in the Last Days*** will focus on the following topics:

- Are You Sealed Tight and Safe?
- How To Stay Steady in Turbulent Times
- Making Sacrifices To Stay Afloat in the Last Days

- Do You Know Who 'Your People' Are?
- Getting God's Personal Instructions for You!
- Do You Have Ears To Hear What the Spirit Is Saying?
- What Happens If You Obey?
- Do Other People's Opinions Bother You?
- Acting With Fearlessness When God Speaks!
- How To Receive the Promise God Made to You!

The Bible records that a worldwide flood swept across the globe during the days of Noah as a means to thoroughly cleanse the earth of all violence and corruption. God prewarned Noah of what was coming and gave him a detailed plan of how to save his family. He was to build an ark, and in that ark, he and his family — and a sampling of all the land animals and birds of the air — would be preserved. According to Genesis 7:17, they literally floated on a sea of destruction.

Today, we're living in a time when we're surrounded by insanity. From the polluted world of politics and decadence of the entertainment world to the twisting of Scripture and the rampant apostasy in the Church, a sea of destruction is all around us. Without question, we're concerned about our kids and our grandkids and what the future holds for them. But just as Noah and his family were lifted and enabled to float on the waters of destruction, God has made a way for us to float on the sea of trouble in these last days. In fact, what destroys others will cause us to be lifted to the highest place — a place of safety and security.

The emphasis of this lesson:

As a believer, you are permanently placed in Christ, which is the safest place in the world to be, and nothing can touch you. Jesus is your ark of supernatural safety and security.

The Ship-Shaped Ruins in Eastern Turkey Are the Real Deal

In 1959, during a routine mapping expedition, a huge, man-made object was discovered in the mountains of Ararat. After dozens of scans and ground-penetrating radar, it was determined that this ship-shaped vessel had three distinct levels and multiple rooms throughout. Amazingly, its dimensions fit the description given by God to Noah in Genesis 6 and thus confirm that this ship is indeed the ruins of Noah's Ark.

Rick and his team traveled to eastern Turkey and filmed a groundbreaking series entitled *Fallen Angels, Giants, Monsters, and the World Before the Flood*, which we highly recommend and can be obtained at **renner.org**. What's interesting is that since their visit, numerous scientific reports have been made confirming that the ruins in the lower mountains of Ararat are indeed the remains of Noah's Ark.

This find is extremely significant for many reasons, but one of the most important ones is linked to what Jesus prophesied in His renowned Olivet Discourse. As He spoke with His disciples concerning the last days, He declared,

> **But as the days of Noe [Noah] were, so shall also the coming of the Son of man be.**
> **— Matthew 24:37**

The original Greek text of this verse reveals that Jesus was literally saying, "What was taking place on the earth just before the Flood will be replicated at the end of the age in connection with My return." Friend, we are living at the end of the age, which is why violence and corruption are flourishing and there are so many bizarre things taking place. These last-of-the-last-days signs are described by Jesus in Matthew 24 and by the apostle Paul in Second Timothy 3, and they are happening in society all around us.

Jesus Is the Only Door to Safety

After fully obeying God's instructions, building the Ark to His specifications, and securing all the animals and food provisions on board, the Bible says, "And they that went in, went in male and female of all flesh, as God had commanded him: and the Lord shut him in. And the flood was forty days upon the earth; and the waters increased, and bare up the ark, and it was lift up above the earth" (Genesis 7:16,17).

Notice it says that "the waters increased and bare up the ark." This literally means that the Ark floated on a sea of destruction. The same flood waters that killed all living creatures on the earth elevated Noah and his family high above all the calamity and chaos.

Also note what God told Noah while he was constructing the Ark. He said, "A window shalt thou make to the ark, and in a cubit shalt thou finish it above; and the door of the ark shalt thou set in the side thereof; with lower, second, and third stories shalt thou make it" (Genesis 6:16). This passage confirms that along with three distinct levels, there was only *one* door. This means that there was only one way to enter the place of safety and security, and if a person didn't come through that single door, they experienced destruction.

Does that sound familiar? It is very similar to what Jesus said in John 14:6: "…I am *the* way, *the* truth, and *the* life: no man cometh unto the Father, but by me." When you come to faith in Christ, repenting of your sins and inviting Him to be your Savior and Lord, you enter the ark of eternal safety! Scripture says, "Only Jesus has the power to save! His name is the only one in all the world that can save anyone" (Acts 4:12 *CEV*). Again, there's no safer place in all the world than to be in Christ.

How Do You Get 'In Christ'?

It may be that you're reading this and wondering how a person gets "in Christ." To answer this question, we turn to Scripture, which says:

> **But what saith it? The word is nigh thee, even in thy mouth, and in thy heart: that is, the word of faith, which we preach; that if thou shalt confess with thy mouth the Lord Jesus, and shalt believe in thine heart that God hath raised him from the dead, thou shalt be saved.**
> **— Romans 10:8,9**

To be clear, when you "confess with thy mouth the Lord Jesus," it means you're submitting your life to Him and allowing Him to call the shots and be your Supreme Master. When you confess with your mouth that Jesus is Lord and believe in your heart that God raised Him from the dead, you are saved. What's interesting is that while the word "saved" certainly describes *eternal salvation* and a place in Heaven, it also indicates the gift of *present deliverance, preservation, protection, healing, and wholeness in this life on earth.*

Romans 10:10 goes on to say, "For with the heart man believeth unto righteousness; and with the mouth confession is made unto salvation." Thus, we see that being *saved* requires two specific actions on our part: a verbal acknowledgment that Jesus is Lord over all, including us, and that

God raised Him from the dead. This lets us know that believing in Jesus privately is not enough; we must make our confession of faith public for our salvation to be complete.

This passage continues by saying, "For the scripture saith, Whosoever believeth on him shall not be ashamed. For there is no difference between the Jew and the Greek: for the same Lord over all is rich unto all that call upon him. For whosoever shall call upon the name of the Lord shall be saved." (Romans 10:11-13). Here again we see the word "saved," the Greek word *sodzo*, which carries the idea of *eternal salvation* as well as *deliverance, preservation, protection, healing, and wholeness in this present life*.

There are no favorites with God — anyone who calls on the name of the Lord and makes Him Supreme Master of his or her life will be saved. In that moment of salvation, the Holy Spirit takes each of us and supernaturally places us into the Body of Christ, which is our ark of refuge, the safest place in the world.

In Christ, We Are Blessed With Everything We Need

Now that we know how to get in Christ, let's look at what the apostle Paul says about being in Christ in Ephesians 1. Interestingly, he begins by saying, "Paul, an apostle of Jesus Christ by the will of God, to the saints which are at Ephesus, and to the faithful ***in Christ Jesus***" (Ephesians 1:1). So in addition to addressing the believers at Ephesus, he also speaks to the faithful in Christ Jesus.

In verse 3, he declares, "Blessed be the God and Father of our Lord Jesus Christ, who hath blessed us with all spiritual blessings in heavenly places ***in Christ***" (Ephesians 1:3). And in verse 4, we learn that we were selected "according as he hath chosen us **in him** before the foundation of the world, that we should be holy and without blame before him in love" (Ephesians 1:4). So the moment we are saved, we are placed *in Christ*, and in that ark of safety, we are blessed with every spiritual blessing imaginable. This passage also reveals that the Father chose each of us *before* the world began — wow!

In all these things, God receives glory! That's what we see in Ephesians 1:6 and 7, which says, "To the praise of the glory of his grace, wherein he hath made us accepted ***in the beloved***. In whom we have redemption through his blood, the forgiveness of sins, according to the riches of his grace." Think about that. In Christ, God *makes us acceptable*, which means we meet His standard and are pleasing to Him. Moreover, in Christ, we are *redeemed through His Blood* — which means Jesus bought us back from Satan's slave market and set us free from his power and the power of sin. In Christ, we also have forgiveness for our sins because of God's immeasurable mercy and grace.

Ephesians 1:11 goes on to tell us that **in Christ**, "…We have obtained an inheritance, being predestinated according to the purpose of him who worketh all things after the counsel of his own will." If you are saved and Jesus Christ is your Lord and Savior, you are tucked away deeply in Him, and you are positioned to receive an inheritance for His sake.

God Has Placed His Seal of Approval on Us

What else happens as a result of being in Christ? Paul said, "In [Christ] whom ye also trusted, after that ye heard the word of truth, the gospel of your salvation: in whom also after that ye believed, ye were sealed with that holy Spirit of promise, which is the earnest of our inheritance until the redemption of the purchased possession, unto the praise of his glory" (Ephesians 1:13,14). There are three key words in this passage you really need to know and understand.

First is the word "salvation," which is the Greek word *soteria*. It's the same word we saw used in Romans 10 translated as "saved." It expresses the idea of *present deliverance, healing, preservation, prosperity, safety, and general welfare*. So not only do you receive eternal salvation the moment you get saved, but also *deliverance, healing, preservation, prosperity, safety, and general welfare* in the here and now.

Next, the Bible says that you were "sealed," which in this instance is the remarkable Greek word *sphragidzo*. It pictures *a seal placed on a package after the product had been thoroughly examined and inspected to make sure it was fully intact and complete*. The seal was proof the product was impeccable. Normally such seals bore the insignia of a wealthy or famous person, which meant that this package was to be treated with tender care. This seal affirmed the owner of the package and guaranteed that the package had sufficient postage paid to make it to its final destination.

The use of this word *sphragidzo* — translated here as "sealed" — means the day you got saved, God placed you in Christ, thoroughly inspected you, and found you to be fully intact and complete! He looked at your bornagain condition and pronounced you as impeccable. He then placed His seal of approval on you, and that seal is His Holy Spirit! How amazing!

The Holy Spirit Is the Downpayment That Guarantees Our Delivery Into Eternity

Ephesians 1:14 adds that the seal of the Holy Spirit is "the earnest of our inheritance…." The word "earnest" here is the Greek word *arrabon*, which is *payment given in advance to guarantee the whole amount will be paid afterward*. It can be translated as *earnest money, an installment, a deposit*, or *a down payment that guarantees full delivery of a promise*. Essentially, it is *a security deposit given by the purchaser to assure confidence and peace to the seller that he will fulfill his promise*.

Taking into account the meanings of these words, here is the *Renner Interpretive Version* (*RIV*) of Ephesians 1:13 and 14:

> **When you were placed in Christ, God stamped you with a special seal and embossed it so deeply that it cannot be broken, erased, rubbed out, wiped out, deleted or removed. That unbreakable seal is the Holy Spirit. Once you were stamped with Him, it meant you had God's approval. He examined the contents of your heart and found nothing flawed or inferior.**
>
> **And because everything was in order, He stamped you with the Holy Spirit, which is His seal of approval. Anyone who has this stamp is headed for special treatment. This seal means you belong to God and no one is to interfere with you as a "package."**
>
> **This "Holy Spirit stamp" means the postage is prepaid to get you all the way to your ultimate destination. That means you can be sure that once your journey with the Lord begins, you are going to make it all the way to where God wants you to go! As good as all of this already seems, it's only the beginning of what God has planned for us.**

Friend, there is no safer place in the world than to be in Christ Jesus! That is where God tucks you away the moment you are saved, and He seals you with His Holy Spirit. Just as Noah and his family could only enter the Ark through one door, Jesus said we can only enter a right relationship with God through Him. He said, "…I am *the* way, *the* truth, and *the* life: no man cometh unto the Father, but by me" (John 14:6).

When you give your life to Jesus, God places you into Christ, and you are sealed into Him. You are also safe in Him, and in these last days, this will enable you to rise above the waters of destruction and sail victoriously through any stormy situation, all the way to your ultimate destination, which is Heaven!

Questions and Answers With Rick Renner

In the program, Rick answered the following question from one of our viewers.

Q. What is your most important purpose in life?

A. "I struggled with that question for many years," Rick said on the program. "I wondered, *Is my purpose ministry? Is it pastoring?* Then I began to ask the Lord, 'What is my purpose? Why am I here?

And what is the most important thing that I can do?' I found the answer in Revelation 4:11, which says:

> Thou art worthy, O Lord, to receive glory and honour and power: for thou hast created all things, and for thy pleasure they are and were created.

"That's it! I said to myself. I finally understood why I am here — and why we are *all* here. It's not so much about what you and I do. Our most important purpose in life is to bring pleasure to the Lord. That is our highest goal and greatest ambition. You and I are created for His pleasure."

In our next lesson, we will focus our attention on how to remain steady in turbulent times.

STUDY QUESTIONS

> Study to shew thyself approved unto God, a workman that
> needeth not to be ashamed, rightly dividing the word of truth.
> — 2 Timothy 2:15

1. When you hear that the remains of Noah's Ark have been found in eastern Turkey and confirmed to be the real deal, how does it affect your faith in God and the reliability of His Word?
2. According to Jesus' words in Matthew 24:1-14 (*and* Mark 13:1-13), what are some of the signs He said we can expect to see before His coming? What did the apostle Paul say the world will be like in the last days in Second Timothy 3:1-9? Are you seeing any of these things take place?
3. Ephesians 1:3 tells us we are blessed "with all spiritual blessings in heavenly places *in Christ*." How is this verse similar to what the Holy Spirit wrote through Peter in Second Peter 1:2-4? Did you know that all this was available to you? How do these promises embolden you to pray and receive all that has been provided to you in Christ?

PRACTICAL APPLICATION

> But be ye doers of the word, and not hearers only, deceiving your own selves.
> —James 1:22

1. Jesus prophesied that what was happening in the days of Noah would be duplicated in the last days before His coming. What do you see taking place in the world today that is similar to the time just before the Flood — especially in the form of *violence* and *corruption*?
2. Romans 10:9 and 10 reveal that to be *saved* requires that we believe in our heart and confess with our mouth that Jesus is Lord over all and that God raised Him from the dead. Have you done this? Are you saved? If not, take time right now to pray and get into the ark of safety — Jesus Christ — by believing in your heart and confessing with your mouth that Jesus Christ is Lord.

LESSON 2

TOPIC
How To Stay Steady in Turbulent Times

SCRIPTURES
1. **Genesis 7:16,17** — And they that went in, went in male and female of all flesh, as God had commanded him: and the Lord shut him in. And the flood was forty days upon the earth; and the waters increased, and bare up the ark, and it was lift up above the earth.
2. **Isaiah 33:6** — And wisdom and knowledge shall be the stability of thy times, and strength of salvation....
3. **Luke 6:47-49** — Whosoever cometh to me, and heareth my sayings, and doeth them, I will shew you to whom he is like: He is like a man which built an house, and digged deep, and laid the foundation on a rock: and when the flood arose, the stream beat vehemently upon that house, and could not shake it: for it was founded upon a rock. But he that heareth, and doeth not, is like a man that without a foundation built an house upon the earth; against which the stream did beat vehemently, and immediately it fell; and the ruin of that house was great.

GREEK WORDS
1. "house" — οἶκος (*oikos*): a house; a family; pictures one's entire life
2. "digged" — σκάπτω (*skapto*): to dig or to dig deeply
3. "deep" — βαθύνω (*bathuno*): deep; to dive deep; to plummet to the depths
4. "laid the foundation" — ἔθηκεν θεμέλιον (*etheken themelion*): from τίθημι (*tithemi*), meaning to establish, to lay, or to place, and almost always used with an architectural connection; and θεμέλιος (*themelios*), which pictures a solidly laid foundation
5. "on" — ἐπί (*epi*): on; directly on; upon
6. "a rock" — τὴν πέτραν (*ten petran*): a definite article with a form of πέτρα (*petra*), meaning a firm, massive, solid rock

7. "flood" — **πλημμύρα** (*plemmura*): a flood, either from a river or sea, but here it pictures a river; a flooding river that covers and overwhelms
8. "stream" — **ποταμός** (*potamos*): a river; a flooding, torrential river or stream
9. "beat vehemently upon" — **προσρήγνυμι** (*prosregnumi*): to break into pieces, to burst, to rend, or to tear apart
10. "for" — **διά** (*dia*): for, on account of, or due to the fact
11. "without a foundation…upon the earth" — **ἐπὶ τὴν γῆν χωρὶς θεμελίου** (*epi ten gen choris themeliou*): directly on the ground, apart from, or without a foundation
12. "stream" — **ποταμός** (*potamos*): a river; a flooding, torrential river or stream
13. "beat vehemently" — **προσρήγνυμι** (*prosregnumi*): to break into pieces, to burst, to rend, or to tear apart

SYNOPSIS

Jesus said, "But as the days of Noah were, so shall also the coming of the Son of man be" (Matthew 24:37). In the original Greek text, this literally means that what was going on at the time just before the Flood will be going on again in the time just before Christ returns. We might even say it will be *a duplicate moment*. The recent rediscovery of the ruins of Noah's ark in the lower Ararat mountains in eastern Turkey is a sobering reminder that a worldwide flood really did take place. And just as things were out-of-the-box bizarre then, they're becoming just as crazy now in our time.

What's interesting is that if you journey down into the flood plain below the mountains where the ruins of the Ark are located, you'll discover the ancient remains of objects known as drogue stones. In this lesson, we will learn the fascinating facts about these huge hewn formations and how their presence confirms that the remains of a ship located in the mountains of Ararat are indeed from Noah's Ark. We'll also discover how they symbolize something we desperately need in our lives to enable us to successfully navigate the turbulent times in which we live.

The emphasis of this lesson:

In addition to being in Christ Jesus — our "ark of safety" — we also need the stabilizing force of God's Word to anchor our lives. His Word acts like the ancient drogue stones that hung from the sides of Noah's Ark and kept it from capsizing in the turbulent wind and waves of the worldwide flood.

What Are Drogue Stones?

Drogue stones were very important in the ancient world of sailing. They were huge pieces of rock that had a hole cut at one end so a rope could be fastened to it, and they were hung from the sides of a ship. Drogue stones were used to slow the vessel down in a storm and to prevent it from capsizing in rough weather. They helped control ships so they wouldn't speed down the slope of a wave and crash into the next one.

Overall, drogue stones provided balance and stability in rough waters and were a feature of nearly all ancient ships. They have been found in places like the Nile River and the Mediterranean, and all surviving examples look identical to the ones found in the lower plains of the Ararat mountain range.

There are some very interesting things about the stones near the site of Noah's Ark. First, they are enormous, with each stone weighing several tons. Although many are now fragments and partially buried, some are still fully intact and easily identifiable as drogue stones. The reason they are so big is because of the size of the Ark. These larger stones were heavier and provided the needed stability for the Ark through the roughest seas ever known.

Another fascinating fact is that on most of the stones, eight crosses have been carved into them, which appears to have been done by early Armenian believers who wanted to memorialize the place in honor of the eight souls that survived the Flood. In fact, the ancient name of the town in which the stones are found is called the Village of Eight.[1]

Why Would Ship Anchors Be Found in Mountains?

Interestingly, there is a trail of over two dozen drogue stones in the area near eastern Turkey in the Ararat mountain range. The question is why would mammoth-sized rock anchors be found in a mountainous region?

They simply do not belong there…unless there was a massive ship in that area at some time.

Think about it. There are no large bodies of water near the mountains of Ararat. Where are the closest seas?

- The Baltic Sea is 1,500 miles away.
- The Mediterranean Sea is 506 miles away.
- The Black Sea is 192 miles away.
- The Caspian Sea is 310 miles away.

So why are there massive drogue stones in the area? And why is a massive ship-shaped formation also there on the lower slopes of the Ararat mountain range? The answer is that there really was a worldwide flood exactly as the Bible tells us in Genesis 6 through 9, and Noah and his family — a family of eight — did sail the Ark through that exact area. It's not a fairytale — it's a fact.

Eventually, the Ark landed nearby on the lower slopes of the Ararat mountains, and if you come to the region today, you can follow the path of drogue stones that lead right up to the place where the Ark came to rest on what is called Mount Judi.[2] As Noah and his family sailed through the area, they began to cut one stone after another. By following the stones, you can determine the direction the Ark sailed right into the lower mountains of Ararat.

Again, these drogue stones hung from the sides of the Ark and brought it stability in the roughest weather the world had ever known with waves beyond our imagination. But because of the drogue stones, the Ark didn't capsize, and all life was preserved.

God's Word Is Our 'Drogue Stones'

After Noah had obeyed God and built the Ark as he had been instructed, the Bible says, "And they that went in, went in male and female of all flesh, as God had commanded him: and the Lord shut him in. And the flood was forty days upon the earth; and the waters increased, and bare up the ark, and it was lift up above the earth" (Genesis 7:16,17).

Amazingly, the same water that decimated everything on the earth is what caused Noah and his family to rise higher and higher and float on the waters of destruction! One reason they were able to stay afloat is because of the massive drogue stones that kept the ship balanced in the middle of the biggest waves the world has ever seen. God knew that Noah needed the weight of those stones to keep them balanced in rough waters.

And just as Noah needed those stones to keep the Ark stable and afloat, we need God's Word to keep us stable and afloat in these turbulent times. Next to the indwelling power of the Holy Spirit, the Word of God is the most important stabilizing force for sailing through the rough waters of these last days. When God's Word is fixed in our lives, it will keep us from capsizing in tough times — even if waters of destruction are all around us.

Isaiah 33:6 says, "And wisdom and knowledge shall be the stability of thy times, and strength of salvation...." God's Word is divine wisdom and knowledge that provides stability to our lives at all times.

What Happens When You Build Your Life on God's Word?

Jesus was — and is — the Word of God in physical, flesh-and-bone form (*see* John 1:14). He had much to say about the importance and power of building your life on the Word — including these priceless insights in Luke 6:47 and 48:

> **Whosoever cometh to me, and heareth my sayings, and doeth them, I will shew you to whom he is like: He is like a man which built an house, and digged deep, and laid the foundation on a rock: and when the flood arose, the stream beat vehemently upon that house, and could not shake it: for it was founded upon a rock.**

There are several key words in this verse deserving of our attention. For example, take the word "house," which is the Greek word *oikos*. It describes *a house* or *a family* and can also pictures *one's entire life*. So, when Jesus talked about a "house," He's actually referring to how a person has built his life.

In this case, this individual has "digged deep, and laid the foundation on a rock" (Luke 6:48). The word "digged" is the Greek word *skapto*, and it means *to dig* or *to dig deeply*. The word "deep" is the Greek word *bathuno*, which means *deep, to dive deep*, or *to plummet to the depths*. Hence, this is a person who is not interested in doing something shallow, but in digging deep and plummeting down to the depths to lay a foundation.

This brings us to the phrase "laid the foundation," which is *etheken themelion* in Greek, from the words *tithemi* and *themelios*. The word *tithemi* means *to establish*, *to lay*, or *to place*, and is almost always used with an architectural connection; and the word *themelios* pictures *a solidly laid foundation*. When we put these words together to form *etheken themelion*, it means *to lay a rock-solid foundation*.

Then Jesus added the words "on a rock." The word "on" here is the Greek word *epi*, which means *on*; *directly on*; or *upon*. And the words "a rock" in Greek is *ten petran*, which is a form of the word *petra*, meaning *a firm, massive, solid rock*, plus the definite article *ten*. By using all these words, we see that this man did not stop digging until he hit solid rock, and once he hit solid rock, he knew he had something he could build upon.

Jesus went on to say, "…And when the flood arose, the stream beat vehemently upon that house, and could not shake it: for it was founded upon a rock" (Luke 6:48). The word "flood" is the Greek word *plemmura*, which describes *a flood, either from a river or sea*. Here, it pictures *a flooding river that covers and overwhelms*. Jesus said this flooding river "arose," which is a form of the Greek word *ginomai*, and it describes *something that happens by surprise and totally takes a person off guard*.

What is being described here is a sudden, unexpected attack from the enemy. It is depicted as a "stream that beat vehemently upon that house." In Greek, the word "stream" is *potamos*, and it describes *a river* or *a flooding, torrential river or stream*. And the phrase "beat vehemently upon" is a translation of the Greek word *prosregnumi*, which means *to break into pieces, to burst, to rend, or to tear apart*.

Don't miss what Jesus is telling us here. He is saying that those who dig deep and plummet to the depths to lay a solid foundation for their life, building upon the rock-solid foundation of His Word, are NOT torn apart or broken into pieces when the enemy suddenly attacks. In other words, when we do what Jesus says to do in His Word, our life is stabilized and firmly established on an unshakable foundation.

What Happens When You Just Hear and DON'T DO the Word?

Those who choose to *not* put into practice what God's Word says experience a very different outcome. Jesus makes the results clear in Luke 6:49:

> **But he that heareth, and doeth not, is like a man that without a foundation built an house upon the earth; against which the stream did beat vehemently, and immediately it fell; and the ruin of that house was great.**

First, notice that this person also heard the Word, but the difference here is that he didn't do what the Word says. One who only hears the Word is like a person who builds his house — or *life* — "without a foundation… upon the earth." In Greek, this phrase literally means *directly on the ground, apart from,* or *without a foundation*.

Those who don't dig deep and build their life on the "rock" of God's Word, are extremely weak and defenseless to the enemy's attacks. Jesus said, "…The stream did beat vehemently, and immediately it fell; and the ruin of that house was great" (Luke 6:49). Again, we see the Greek word *potamos* — translated as "stream" — and it describes *a flooding, torrential river or stream*, and it, too, *beat vehemently* against this man's life. The phrase "beat vehemently" is the Greek word *prosregnumi*, which means *to break into pieces, to burst, to rend,* or *to tear apart*.

Are you seeing the facts about these two people who are building their life?

- BOTH hear God's Word.
- BOTH are building their life.
- BOTH experience an overwhelming flood of attacks from the enemy.

However, only the one who builds his life on God's Word — ONLY THE DOER OF THE WORD — is unscathed by the flood of attack against his life. The man whose house survived the roughest conditions was the one who had the Word of God stabilizing his life. Without the Word, we have no depth, we have no stability, we have no anchor, and when the storms of life come, we are quickly swept away.

God's Word Is Our Supernatural Stabilizer!

Make no mistake: The Bible is a book like no other book in the world. It contains the mind of God, the condition of man, the way of salvation, the judgment of sinners, and the happiness of believers. Its doctrines are holy, its truths are binding, its histories are true, and its decisions are unchangeable.

Read it — to be wise.

Believe it — to be safe.

Practice it — to be holy.

It is the traveler's map, the pilot's compass, and the soldier's sword. It should fill your memory, rule your heart, and guide your feet. Read it slowly, read it frequently, and read it prayerfully. Your obedience to it is your highest responsibility.

Just as Noah's Ark had drogue stones, the Word of God is the anchor you must have to remain stable and balanced in these turbulent last days. When God's Word is in your life and you're *doing* what it says, the Word acts like those drogue stones, which hung from the sides of Noah's Ark. This is why Rick starts every day of his life by reading the Bible.

Friend, we're living on a sea of destruction and it's all around us. As believers, we are in Christ, which is the safest place to be, but we also need the Word of God to steady us in difficult times. We encourage you to make God's Word the highest priority in your life. And as you do, everything will rise to a new, higher level.

Questions and Answers With Rick Renner

In the program, Rick answered the following question from one of our viewers.

Q. Do you believe the news?

A. Rick said, "Well, when the star appeared to announce the birth of Jesus, people interpreted the phenomenon differently. For example, if you lived in the East like the Magi, they believed it was the announcement that the Great King who had been prophesied for centuries was finally born. But in the Western world, they saw the same star and believed it was a divine sign that Emperor Octavian was god. How the people interpreted the news depended on where they were.

"Likewise, today, you can hear a single news story, but it's interpreted differently according to who is giving you the news. So when I listen to the news, I don't just listen to it from one source — I listen to all sides. Most importantly, I've got my spiritual ears open to hear what the Holy Spirit is saying. He helps me to interpret what the truth is about what I'm hearing. If we'll open our ears to hear the Holy Spirit, He will help us to discern the truth of what we're hearing."

In our next lesson, we will learn the importance of making sacrifices in order to stay afloat in turbulent times.

STUDY QUESTIONS

> **Study to shew thyself approved unto God, a workman that needeth not to be ashamed, rightly dividing the word of truth.**
> **— 2 Timothy 2:15**

1. The weather and sea conditions experienced by Noah and his family were unlike anything anyone has ever gone through. Have you ever thought about the size of the waves, the force of the winds, and the roar of the thunder they endured? What do you think that may have been like? How might such conditions have challenged your faith?

2. Just as Noah needed drogue stones to keep the Ark stable and afloat, we need God's Word to keep us stable and afloat in these turbulent times. What can you expect to happen in your life as you regularly read and study the Bible? Consider what God promises you in these verses:
   - Psalm 19:7-11
   - Psalm 119:11,105,130
   - Hebrews 4:12
   - James 1:21
   - Psalm 119:9; John 17:17; Ephesians 5:26

3. The man in Jesus' story who heard the Word but didn't DO the Word experienced disaster in his life. What else does God tell us about being a DOER of the Word in James 1:22-25 and Joshua 1:7 and 8?

PRACTICAL APPLICATION

> **But be ye doers of the word, and not hearers only, deceiving your own selves.**
> **— James 1:22**

1. Jesus said those who dig deep and lay a solid foundation for their life upon the rock-solid foundation of His Word are NOT torn apart or

broken into pieces when the enemy attacks. Be honest — does this describe you? Are you building your life daily on the truth of God's Word? If not, what are you building your life on? What are you reading, watching, and listening to for knowledge, wisdom, direction, and strength in your life? Is it infusing you with hope and peace?

2. If what you're doing isn't working, you need to make some changes. Pause and pray, "Holy Spirit, what can I do to get more of God's Word in me on a regular basis? What do I need to let go of to have more time to feed my spirit the truth of Scripture?" Be still and listen. What is the Holy Spirit saying to you?

---

[1] "Village of Eight" gives clues to true resting place of Noah's ark – POD," Wyatt Archaeological Research, accessed 12/16/23, https://www.youtube.com/watch?v=6n01QA0B6Vk&t=311s

[2] Ibid.

LESSON 3

TOPIC
Making Sacrifices To Stay Afloat in the Last Days

SCRIPTURES

1. **Matthew 24:37** — But as the days of Noe [Noah] were, so shall also the coming of the Son of man be.
2. **Genesis 7:16,17** — And they that went in, went in male and female of all flesh, as God had commanded him: and the Lord shut him in. And the flood was forty days upon the earth; and the waters increased, and bare up the ark, and it was lift up above the earth.
3. **Genesis 8:18-22** — And Noah went forth, and his sons, and his wife, and his sons' wives with him: every beast, every creeping thing, and every fowl, and whatsoever creepeth upon the earth, after their kinds, went forth out of the ark. And Noah built an altar unto the Lord; and took of every clean beast, and of every clean fowl, and offered

burnt offerings on the altar. And the Lord smelled a sweet savour; and the Lord said in his heart, I will not again curse the ground any more for man's sake; for the imagination of man's heart is evil from his youth; neither will I again smite any more every thing living, as I have done. While the earth remaineth, seedtime and harvest, and cold and heat, and summer and winter, and day and night shall not cease.

4. **Genesis 9:8-17** — And God spake unto Noah, and to his sons with him, saying, And I, behold, I establish my covenant with you, and with your seed after you; And with every living creature that is with you, of the fowl, of the cattle, and of every beast of the earth with you; from all that go out of the ark, to every beast of the earth. And I will establish my covenant with you, neither shall all flesh be cut off any more by the waters of a flood; neither shall there any more be a flood to destroy the earth. And God said, This is the token of the covenant which I make between me and you and every living creature that is with you, for perpetual generations: I do set my bow in the cloud, and it shall be for a token of a covenant between me and the earth. And it shall come to pass, when I bring a cloud over the earth, that the bow shall be seen in the cloud: And I will remember my covenant, which is between me and you and every living creature of all flesh; and the waters shall no more become a flood to destroy all flesh. And the bow shall be in the cloud; and I will look upon it, that I may remember the everlasting covenant between God and every living creature of all flesh that is upon the earth. And God said unto Noah, This is the token of the covenant, which I have established between me and all flesh that is upon the earth.

5. **Romans 12:1** — I beseech you therefore, brethren, by the mercies of God, that ye present your bodies a living sacrifice, holy, acceptable unto God, which is your reasonable service.

6. **Psalm 141:2** — Let my prayer be set forth before thee as incense; and the lifting up of my hands as the evening sacrifice.

7. **Hebrews 13:15,16** (*NKJV*) — Therefore by Him let us continually offer the sacrifice of praise to God, that is, the fruit of our lips, giving thanks to His name. But do not forget to do good and to share, for with such sacrifices God is well pleased.

8. **Philippians 4:18** — But I have all, and abound: I am full, having received of Epaphroditus the things which were sent from you, an odour of a sweet smell, a sacrifice acceptable, wellpleasing to God.

GREEK WORDS

There were no Greek words shown on the program for this lesson.

SYNOPSIS

If you were to travel to the lower mountains of Ararat in eastern Turkey today, you would see for yourself a massive ship-shaped object encased in the earth — an object with the exact dimensions of Noah's Ark as described in Genesis 6. Rather than land atop Mount Ararat as many have mistakenly thought (the present-day Mount Ararat is a stratovolcano with two prominent peaks), the Bible says, "…The ark rested in the seventh month, on the seventeenth day of the month, upon the mountains of Ararat" (Genesis 8:4).

Since Rick and his team went to Turkey and filmed his series *Fallen Angels, Giants, Monsters, and the World Before the Flood*, a number of scientists have recently confirmed that the ship-shaped remains on the lower slope of Mount Judi are indeed the ruins of Noah's Ark. Additionally, the massive drogue stones found strewn throughout the plains below the ship's remains are even further proof that the vessel is indeed Noah's Ark.

But there's something else at the site that adds even more credence to the findings, and that is the enormous stone altar, which many scholars and researchers believe is the very altar where Noah offered his sacrifices to the Lord when he and his family disembarked from the Ark. His actions are an example of the importance of making sacrifices to God. And while we no longer offer Him animals on an altar, there are specific ways in the New Testament that we are instructed to live a life of sacrifice to Him.

The emphasis of this lesson:

The five specific ways in which we are to live a life of sacrifice to God include: the sacrifice of our body; the sacrifice of prayer; the sacrifice of praise; the sacrifice of serving others; and the sacrifice of our finances. When we sacrifice to God, it draws His presence, His power, and His promises into our lives.

Noah and His Family Floated on the Waters of Destruction

What did Noah, his family, and all the animals do once the Ark was completed? Scripture says, "And they that went in, went in male and female of all flesh, as God had commanded him: and the Lord shut him in. And the flood was forty days upon the earth; and the waters increased, and bare up the ark, and it was lift up above the earth" (Genesis 7:16,17).

Imagine that! The same flood waters that annihilated everything on earth are what caused Noah and his family to rise above the chaos and literally float on the waters of destruction! They listened to and obeyed God's instructions, entering that one door into the Ark, and their lives were protected and preserved.

In the same way, when we give our life to Jesus, God places us deep inside Christ, who is our "Ark of Safety." And if we will continue to read His Word and *do* what it says, it will serve to stabilize and steady us amid turbulent times — just as the drogue stones brought balance and stability to Noah's Ark. Although there is destruction all around us, we can sail through these last days victoriously by building our life on the rock-solid foundation of God's Word.

Sacrificing to God Was the Top Priority for Noah

In addition to the ruins of Noah's ark and the dozens of drogue stones positioned throughout the area, there is also a massive sacrificial stone near the place where the Ark landed on Mount Judi. The Kurdish people, who have lived at this site for thousands of years on the nearby slopes, state that this stone is the very altar upon which Noah offered his first sacrifice after exiting the Ark.

This stone from ancient times has a man-made blood channel cut right across the top to direct blood to flow off the sides of it. Visually, you can see it was the place where animals were obviously sacrificed. If this truly is the stone altar upon which Noah and his family made sacrifices, it is the most ancient altar of all the altars in the world. Thus, it is likely the very altar we read about in Genesis 8:18-20:

> **And Noah went forth, and his sons, and his wife, and his sons' wives with him: Every beast, every creeping thing, and every**

> fowl, and whatsoever creepeth upon the earth, after their kinds, went forth out of the ark.
>
> And Noah builded an altar unto the Lord; and took of every clean beast, and of every clean fowl, and offered burnt offerings on the altar.

Notice that the first thing Noah did after exiting the Ark was to build an altar and offer sacrifices to the Lord. Offering animals started with God Himself when He performed the very first sacrifice in Genesis 3:21. He used the animal skins to cover Adam and Eve's nakedness after they sinned. Through the sacrifices Noah offered, he and his family worshiped the Lord and expressed thanks to Him for carrying them through the Flood.

Noah Built an Altar to 'Mercy'

There is something else that's interesting in Genesis 8:20. When it says, "And Noah builded an altar unto the Lord," the Hebrew word for "Lord" is *Hashem*, which is the word for *Mercy*. Hence, we could translate this verse to say, "Noah built an altar unto *Mercy*." God had certainly been merciful to Noah and his family, and Noah knew it.

Think about it: They had been on the Ark for about a year, floating on the waters of destruction. When the Ark finally came to rest in the lower mountains of Ararat, Noah and his family offered their first sacrifice to God, and they called Him the Merciful One. They built an altar unto mercy, and they wanted to thank God for the victory they had experienced.

When Noah and his family exited the Ark, even though the earth was dry, it would not have been the prettiest picture. If you've seen the aftermath of a local flood on the news, you know that floods can be very destructive. Well, just imagine what the surroundings might look like after a global flood has destroyed the face of the earth. When Noah stepped out of the Ark with his family, everything was a mess.

Even today, on top of Mount Judi where the ruins of Noah's Ark lie, the slope quickly becomes covered with a muddy sludge when it rains. In fact, there is such a sea of mud that it is difficult to walk upon it. It's very possible that when Noah stepped out of the Ark and saw the post-Flood world, he said to himself, *Is this what I've inherited? This muddy mess looks nothing like the earth did before.* In that moment, Noah knew he needed God's help.

Accordingly, he built an altar and offered sacrifices to *Hashem*, the God of *mercy*. As he and his family thanked the Lord for preserving their lives from the cataclysmic destruction that engulfed the earth, they also appealed to His mercy to help them make it in the new world.

How Did God Respond to Noah's Act of Worship?

It's really important to see how the sacrifices made by Noah and his family touched the heart of God. The Bible tells us in Genesis 8:21 and 22:

> **And the Lord smelled a sweet savour; and the Lord said in his heart, I will not again curse the ground any more for man's sake; for the imagination of man's heart is evil from his youth; neither will I again smite any more everything living, as I have done.**

> **While the earth remaineth, seedtime and harvest, and cold and heat, and summer and winter, and day and night shall not cease.**

God was so blessed by the sacrifice that it caused Him to bless Noah and his family and to make a promise to them and all future generations that He would never again destroy the entire earth by a global flood. The sign of this covenant promise and its conditions are made clear in Genesis 9:8-17:

> **And God spake unto Noah, and to his sons with him, saying, And I, behold, I establish my covenant with you, and with your seed after you; and with every living creature that is with you, of the fowl, of the cattle, and of every beast of the earth with you; from all that go out of the ark, to every beast of the earth.**

> **And I will establish my covenant with you; neither shall all flesh be cut off any more by the waters of a flood; neither shall there any more be a flood to destroy the earth.**

> **And God said, This is the token of the covenant which I make between me and you and every living creature that is with you, for perpetual generations: I do set my bow in the cloud, and it shall be for a token of a covenant between me and the earth.**

> And it shall come to pass, when I bring a cloud over the earth, that the bow shall be seen in the cloud: And I will remember my covenant, which is between me and you and every living creature of all flesh; and the waters shall no more become a flood to destroy all flesh.
>
> And the bow shall be in the cloud; and I will look upon it, that I may remember the everlasting covenant between God and every living creature of all flesh that is upon the earth.
>
> And God said unto Noah, This is the token of the covenant, which I have established between me and all flesh that is upon the earth.

Amazingly, this detailed covenant promise spoken by God was sparked by the sacrifice Noah and his family made. This gives us a glimpse of how God will respond to us as we offer our sacrifices to Him. Indeed, when you bring a sacrifice to God, it brings His presence, His power, and His promises right into your life!

Five Kinds of Sacrifices We Make to the Lord

It appears that the word "sacrifice" is a compound of two words — one meaning *sacred* and the other meaning *to make*. Thus, in the purest sense, the word "sacrifice" means *to make sacred*. In the times of the Old Testament, a *sacrifice* was most often an offering made to God by killing and burning some animal upon an altar. This act was done as an acknowledgment of His supreme power and providence, to make atonement for sin, to receive His favor, or to express thankfulness for all His blessings.1

A careful study of the New Testament reveals that there are five kinds of sacrifices that we as Christians are to bring to God as a form of worship.

Sacrifice Number 1: The Sacrifice of the Body

The first way in which we worship God is through *the sacrifice of our body*. Writing under the inspiration of the Holy Spirit, the apostle Paul said:

> I beseech you therefore, brethren, by the mercies of God, that ye present your bodies a living sacrifice, holy, acceptable unto God, which is your reasonable service.
> — Romans 12:1

In Romans 12:1, God calls on us to present our bodies as *a living sacrifice*. In Greek, the word "present" here means *to place at God's disposal*; *to surrender*; *to present as a special offering to God*; or *to dedicate once and for all*. This is a sacrifice from which we are to never back away from, never retreat.

Essentially, we are to give our bodies to the Lord once and for all as instruments that He can use. He wants those who belong wholly to Him to lay themselves on the altar — to *stay* on the altar of their own free will — and to remain there as a "living sacrifice." We are to be completely surrendered to Him, dedicated to His purpose, living entirely for Him — *24 hours a day, 7 days a week*.

By using this word in Romans 12:1, Paul is telling each of us to *officially dedicate ourselves — once and for all, forever — to the plans and purposes of God*. It is a sacrifice never to be retracted, and one that we are called to offer to God *daily* — especially in these times when we are surrounded by such a sea of confusion. This is a sweet-smelling savor to God!

Sacrifice Number 2: The Sacrifice of Prayer

Next to reading and studying God's Word, *prayer* is another vital practice that breathes life into our relationship with God. Prayer is communicating with God — plain and simple. In Psalm 141:2, David said:

> **Let my prayer be set forth before thee as incense and the lifting up of my hands as the evening sacrifice.**

The reason prayer is called a sacrifice is because sometimes it's really difficult to pray. Most will agree that when we are surrounded by things like relationship challenges, financial deficits, and sickness, the last thing we feel like doing is praying. Thus, when we pray to God during trials and troubles, it is a sacrifice that is a sweet savor to Him.

Revelation 8:3 and 4 likens our prayers to God as sweet-smelling incense. It says, "And another angel came and stood at the altar, having a golden censer; and there was given unto him much incense, that he should offer it with the prayers of all saints upon the golden altar which was before the throne. And the smoke of the incense, which came with the prayers of the saints, ascended up before God...."

When you come to the altar of God and begin to pray and call upon the Lord, like incense, your prayers come into God's nostrils, and they are a sweet aroma to Him. In fact, it is so pleasing to Him that He wants to come to where you are. Thus, the sacrifice of prayer brings the presence of God, the power of God, and the promise of God. To stay afloat in these last days, we must stay in prayer. This, too, is a sweet-smelling savor to God!

Sacrifice Number 3: The Sacrifice of Praise

A third type of sacrifice we are called to bring to God is *a sacrifice of praise*. Hebrews 13:15 (*NKJV*) says, "Therefore by Him let us continually offer the sacrifice of praise to God, that is, the fruit of our lips, giving thanks to His name." The word "praise" is a translation of a Greek word that depicts *audible expressions of praise*.

Because it is connected to "sacrifice," the message is clear that it can be very sacrificial to offer praise to God at times. Let's face it, if you're in a tough spot in life, you usually don't "feel" like offering praise to God, yet you can push your soul and flesh to the side and choose to do it anyway. In such moments, your praise is indeed a "sacrificial offering" that you brought to the Lord, and it is a sweet-smelling fragrance to Him!

Sacrifice Number 4: The Sacrifice of Serving Others

Immediately after we are instructed to give God a sacrifice of praise, we are told about a fourth kind of sacrifice we are to bring Him, and it is *the sacrifice of serving others*. Hebrews 13:16 (*NKJV*) says:

> **But do not forget to do good and to share, for with such sacrifices God is well pleased.**

When your flesh doesn't want to serve anyone, but you decide you're going to do it anyway, it is a sweet-smelling offering to which God is attracted. As we serve God and others, our personal sacrifices arise like sacrificial incense to Heaven, where God receives an aroma of priestly service that is well-pleasing to Him. In these last days, we need to be ready to serve people who are in trouble — and it may be a sacrifice to do it.

Sacrifice Number 5: The Sacrifice of Our Finances

As believers, we are also to bring financial gifts to the Lord that are sacrificial for us to give. In Philippians, we read that the Philippian believers had sent a sacrificial financial gift to Paul for his ministry. Paul told them:

> **But I have all, and abound: I am full, having received of Epaphroditus the things which were sent from you, an odour of a sweet smell, a sacrifice acceptable, wellpleasing to God.**
> **— Philippians 4:18**

Paul says financial sacrifices are "well-pleasing." God finds it pleasurable when believers give sacrificially, and when we do, He throws open the doors, rolls out the red carpet, and embraces both the giver and the gift! In these last days, we need to financially stay afloat — so we need to continually give sacrificial financial gifts to the Lord that He will multiply back to us! This is a sweet-smelling savor to God!

Just as Noah knew he needed to offer a sacrifice to God to receive His help, if we will bring these five sacrifices to God, it will guarantee His presence and power in our life and activate His promises in our situation — whatever it may be.

Questions and Answers With Rick Renner

In the program, Rick answered the following question from one of our viewers.

Q. Who has played the greatest spiritual role in your life?

A. Rick answered, "Many people have made spiritual impartations into my life, including several friends and many wonderful pastors along the way. But no one has made a greater impartation into my life than my mother, Erlita Renner, who today is in Heaven.

"What my mother poured into my life day in and day out is still working in me today. When I was a child, she would lay by me every night and read the Scriptures to me and talk to me about my soul. She often explained the need to give my life to Jesus, which is why I gave my life to Him at a very early age.

"Moreover, my mother would talk to me about the privilege of serving God and serving people. It is for that reason I love people today and believe serving them is the greatest honor that has been assigned to my life. All these things and so much more are the result of what my mother deposited inside me."

STUDY QUESTIONS

> **Study to shew thyself approved unto God, a workman that needeth not to be ashamed, rightly dividing the word of truth.**
> — 2 Timothy 2:15

1. According to Genesis 9:8-17, with whom did God establish his covenant after the Flood, and what divine promise came with it? Had you ever seen that before?

2. What new insights did you learn about the massive, sacrificial stone altar near the site of the Ark's landing on Mount Judi? How about the importance of sacrifice?

3. When you think about the *mercy* of God, what scriptures come to mind? The fact of the matter is that we are alive today because of God's mercy. If you've not studied the Word to learn about God's mercy, now is a great time! Here are a few key verses to help you get started:

   - Psalm 34:8; 145:3
   - Lamentations 3:22,23
   - Joel 2:12,13; Daniel 9:9; Deuteronomy 4:31
   - Titus 3:3-7
   - James 2:13
   - Matthew 5:7 and Luke 6:36
   - Micah 6:8

PRACTICAL APPLICATION

> **But be ye doers of the word, and not hearers only, deceiving your own selves.**
> — James 1:22

1. The first thing Noah did after exiting the Ark was to build an altar to the Lord and offer sacrifices to Him for His mercy in protecting and preserving him and his family. Take a few moments to look back over your life. What are some of the most memorable ways in which God has shown you and your family mercy? Why not take some time right now to thank Him and praise Him for His kindness to you.

2. Considering pictures and news reports you've seen regarding the aftermath of floods and tsunamis, what do you think the earth looked like after a global flood — caused by both torrential rains and earthquake activity that forced water to gush from below?
3. Take a moment and jot down the five kinds of sacrifices that we as Christians are to bring to God as a form of worship. Which are easier for you to offer to God and seem to flow from you almost effortlessly? Which form of sacrifice do you find hardest to carry out? Why?

---

[1] Adapted from *American Dictionary of the English Language*, s.v. "sacrifice," 1828 (Foundation for America Christian Education; San Francisco, CA: 1967, 1995).

LESSON 4

TOPIC
Do You Know Who 'Your People' Are?

SCRIPTURES
1. **Genesis 7:16,17** — And they that went in, went in male and female of all flesh, as God had commanded him: and the Lord shut him in. And the flood was forty days upon the earth; and the waters increased, and bare up the ark, and it was lift up above the earth.
2. **Genesis 6:17-22** — And, behold, I, even I, do bring a flood of waters upon the earth, to destroy all flesh, wherein is the breath of life, from under heaven; and every thing that is in the earth shall die. But with thee will I establish my covenant; and thou shalt come into the ark, thou, and thy sons, and thy wife, and thy sons' wives with thee. And of every living thing of all flesh, two of every sort shalt thou bring into the ark, to keep them alive with thee; they shall be male and female. Of fowls after their kind, and of cattle after their kind, of every creeping thing of the earth after his kind, two of every sort shall come unto thee, to keep them alive. And take thou unto thee of all food that is eaten, and thou shalt gather it to thee; and it shall be for food for thee, and for them. Thus did Noah; according to all that God commanded him, so did he.

3. **Genesis 7:1,6-11** — And the Lord said unto Noah, Come thou and all thy house into the ark; for thee have I seen righteous before me in this generation.... And Noah was six hundred years old when the flood of waters was upon the earth. And Noah went in, and his sons, and his wife, and his sons' wives with him, into the ark, because of the waters of the flood. Of clean beasts, and of beasts that are not clean, and of fowls, and of every thing that creepeth upon the earth, there went in two and two unto Noah into the ark, the male and the female, as God had commanded Noah. And it came to pass after seven days, that the waters of the flood were upon the earth. In the six hundredth year of Noah's life, in the second month, the seventeenth day of the month, the same day were all the fountains of the great deep broken up, and the windows of heaven were opened.
4. **Genesis 7:13** — In the selfsame day entered Noah, and Shem, and Ham, and Japheth, the sons of Noah, and Noah's wife, and the three wives of his sons with them, into the ark.
5. **Genesis 8:13-16,18** — And it came to pass in the six hundredth and first year, in the first month, the first day of the month, the waters were dried up from off the earth: and Noah removed the covering of the ark, and looked, and, behold, the face of the ground was dry. And in the second month, on the seven and twentieth day of the month, was the earth dried. And God spake unto Noah, saying, Go forth of the ark, thou, and thy wife, and thy sons, and thy sons' wives with thee.... And Noah went forth, and his sons, and his wife, and his sons' wives with him.
6. **Genesis 9:1** — And God blessed Noah and his sons, and said unto them, Be fruitful, and multiply, and replenish the earth.
7. **Genesis 9:8,9** — And God spake unto Noah, and to his sons with him, saying, And I, behold, I establish my covenant with you [plural], and with your seed after you.
8. **Genesis 9:18,19** — And the sons of Noah, that went forth of the ark, were Shem, and Ham, and Japheth.... These are the three sons of Noah: and of them was the whole earth overspread.
9. **Romans 12:5** — So we, being many, are one body in Christ, and every one members one of another.
10. **Ephesians 4:25** — ...For we are members one of another.
11. **Galatians 6:10** — As we have therefore opportunity, let us do good unto all men, especially unto them who are of the household of faith.

12. **Hebrews 10:24,25** — And let us consider one another to provoke unto love and to good works: Not forsaking the assembling of ourselves together, as the manner of some is; but exhorting one another....

13. **Ecclesiastes 4:9-12** — Two are better than one; because they have a good reward for their labour. For if they fall, the one will lift up his fellow: but woe to him that is alone when he falleth; for he hath not another to help him up. Again, if two lie together, then they have heat: but how can one be warm alone? And if one prevail against him, two shall withstand him; and a threefold cord is not quickly broken.

GREEK WORDS

1. "especially" — **μάλιστα** (*malista*): especially, particularly, or most of all
2. "household" — **οἰκείους** (*oikeious*): one's own house; a domestic unit that is closely linked; those who adhere to or who belong to the same group; kindred
3. "consider" — **κατανοέω** (*katanoeo*): to thoroughly consider; to think something through from the top to the bottom; to deeply ponder; pictures a person engaged in focused and concentrated consideration; it is the idea of mulling something over; to carefully contemplate a matter; to ponder and carefully look at a particular issue; to examine and fully study a subject; to contemplate
4. "provoke" — **παροξυσμός** (*paroxusmos*): prodding and impelling a person to do something; to call into combat; to provoke
5. "exhorting" — **παρακαλέω** (*parakaleo*): a compound of **παρα** (*para*) and **καλέω** (*kaleo*); the preposition **παρα** (*para*) means alongside, and **καλέω** (*kaleo*) means I call; as a compound, it means to draw alongside someone else to appeal or to call out to them; to encourage or to exhort; to console someone else; to ignite someone to action by appealing to them; used by the military to denote a commander who charged and exhorted troops to face battles bravely and to fight to victory

SYNOPSIS

Noah really lived, and with the help of his family, he built an Ark just as the Lord had instructed him. The remains of that mammoth ship are located on Mount Judi, which is in the lower level of the Ararat mountains in eastern Turkey. What's interesting is that this area was once known as the ancient region of Urartu, where the Garden of Eden is believed to have been originally located. Since 1959, scientists and researchers have studied this site, conducting numerous ERT scans and using ground-penetrating radar to reveal the dimensions of the ship-shaped vessel submerged in the mud.

It took Noah and his family nearly 100 years to build the Ark. The Bible says, "And they that went in, went in male and female of all flesh, as God had commanded him: and the Lord shut him in. And the flood was forty days upon the earth; and the waters increased, and bare up the ark, and it was lift up above the earth" (Genesis 7:16,17). Amazingly, Noah and his family literally floated on the sea of destruction! And that is what God wants us to do in these last-of-the-last days.

Although we are surrounded by a rising flood of trouble, we are permanently hidden in Christ Jesus — our "Ark of safety" (*see* Colossians 3:3). And just because the world is losing its mind and beginning to capsize, that doesn't mean we have to go under. We have been given the stabilizing power of God's Word, and as we do what it says, we can rise above the craziness and sail through these turbulent times safe and sound.

The emphasis of this lesson:

From the start, God made a covenant with Noah, his wife, his sons, and his sons' wives. All eight people worked together as a unified team to accomplish God's will. In the same way, we each need a family of faith — people with a kindred spirit — to help us do what God has called us to do.

The Task of Preserving and Rebuilding Was Too Big for Noah Alone

In our last lesson, we learned about the massive stone altar found on top of Mount Judi, which is very near to where Noah's Ark landed in the lower mountains of eastern Turkey. Interestingly, the settlement where the altar is located is known as the Village of the Eight. Scholars and researchers believe that that sacrificial stone was indeed used by Noah and his family to make their sacrifices to God — making it the oldest altar in the world.

Along with the massive stone altar, there is a small building, which is an old church that was built on the ruins of a very ancient house that is thousands of years old. It stands in the flood plain just below the Ark's remains, and it was converted into a church by the Byzantines to memorialize the site as the very place where Noah lived, planted a vineyard, and began farming after the Flood.

Keep in mind that what Noah did, he didn't do alone. His wife, his sons, and his sons' wives all helped him in the building of the Ark, caring for the animals, and replenishing the earth after the Flood. He and his family worked together as a team to accomplish the monumental task of preserving and rebuilding. They serve as a reminder that what God has called us to do in these last days we cannot do alone. We need the help of others who share in the vision and in the work that needs to be done.

From the Beginning, God Called Noah and His Whole Family

The Bible tells us that in the days of Noah, the earth became filled with violence and corruption, "And God saw that the wickedness of man was great in the earth, and that every imagination of the thoughts of his heart was only evil continually" (Genesis 6:5). This so grieved God's heart that He decided to cleanse the earth by a worldwide flood.

"But Noah found favor with the Lord" (Genesis 6:8 *NLT*), and because of that favor, God revealed to Noah what was about to take place before it happened. In Genesis 6:17 and 18, He said, "And, behold, I, even I, do bring a flood of waters upon the earth, to destroy all flesh, wherein is the breath of life, from under heaven; and every thing that is in the earth shall die. But with thee will I establish my covenant; and thou shalt come into the ark, thou, and thy sons, and thy wife, and thy sons' wives with thee."

Did you catch the latter part of verse 18? God didn't just make a covenant with Noah — He made a covenant with Noah and his wife and his sons and their wives. From the beginning, this was a family affair — all eight people working as a unified team to accomplish God's will.

The Lord went on to say, "And of every living thing of all flesh, two of every sort shalt thou bring into the ark, to keep them alive with thee; they shall be male and female. Of fowls after their kind, and of cattle after their kind, of every creeping thing of the earth after his kind, two of every sort shall come unto thee, to keep them alive. And take thou unto thee of all food that is eaten, and thou shalt gather it to thee; and it shall be for food for thee, and for them" (Genesis 6:19-21). Note that when God said, "Keep them alive with *thee*," and "Take unto *thee* of all food that is eaten," the word "thee" is plural, referring to everyone in the family.

Noah and his family members obeyed all the instructions they were given. Scripture says, "Thus did Noah; according to all that God commanded him, so did he" (Genesis 6:22).

Noah and His Entire 'Team' Entered and Exited the Ark Together

If we crunch the numbers, it appears that the building of the Ark took approximately 100 years. When it was completed, the Bible says, "And the Lord said unto Noah, Come thou and all thy house into the ark; for thee have I seen righteous before me in this generation.... And Noah was six hundred years old when the flood of waters was upon the earth. And Noah went in, and his sons, and his wife, and his sons' wives with him, into the ark, because of the waters of the flood" (Genesis 7:1,6,7).

Here again, we see the emphasis on the fact that Noah and his *entire family unit* went into the Ark together. They were in covenant together, they built the Ark together, and they entered the Ark together. Meanwhile, the animals also began to make their way into the Ark. Scripture says, "Of clean beasts, and of beasts that are not clean, and of fowls, and of every thing that creepeth upon the earth, there went in two and two unto Noah into the ark, the male and the female, as God had commanded Noah" (Genesis 7:8,9).

It's very interesting to note how precise the Bible documents each detail concerning when everyone got on the Ark, when the rain started, and exactly how old Noah was when it all took place. The Bible says:

> **And it came to pass after seven days, that the waters of the flood were upon the earth. In the six hundredth year of Noah's life, in the second month, the seventeenth day of the month, the same day were all the fountains of the great deep broken up, and the windows of heaven were opened.... In the selfsame day entered Noah, and Shem, and Ham, and Japheth, the sons of Noah, and Noah's wife, and the three wives of his sons with them, into the ark.**
> **— Genesis 7:10,11,13**

It is with the same meticulous documentation that we are told exactly when the Flood ended and when everyone disembarked from the Ark. The Bible says:

> **And it came to pass in the six hundredth and first year, in the first month, the first day of the month, the waters were dried up from off the earth: and Noah removed the covering of the ark, and looked, and, behold, the face of the ground was dry. And in the second month, on the seven and twentieth day of the month, was the earth dried. And God spake unto Noah, saying, Go forth of the ark, thou, and thy wife, and thy sons, and thy sons' wives with thee.... And Noah went forth, and his sons, and his wife, and his sons' wives with him.**
> **— Genesis 8:13-16,18**

Once more, we see an emphasis placed on Noah's entire family. Rather than just say "Noah left the Ark," God purposely includes the fact that all eight people exited at the same time. We see this same emphasis made when God pronounced a blessing on Noah and his family and explained the covenant He made with them. Scripture says, "And God blessed Noah and his sons, and said unto them, Be fruitful, and multiply, and replenish the earth.... And God spake unto Noah, and to his sons with him, saying, And I, behold, I establish my covenant with you [plural], and with your seed after you.... And the sons of Noah, that went forth of the ark, were Shem, and Ham, and Japheth.... These are the three sons of Noah: and of them was the whole earth overspread" (Genesis 9:1,8,9,18,19).

We Need the Help and Strength of Others

The point in all this is that God did not call Noah to do everything on his own. He called Noah AND his wife, his sons, and his sons' wives to accomplish His will. In the same way, you are not called to do your God-assignment alone. There are many people alongside you who are waiting and wanting to help. As believers, we are all a part of the Body of Christ. Scripture says:

> **So we, being many, are one body in Christ, and every one members one of another.**
> **— Romans 12:5**

And in Ephesians, Paul wrote:

...For we are members one of another.

— Ephesians 4:25

Friend, you were never meant to fly solo for Jesus. You were meant to team up with others, and as things grow increasingly bizarre and challenging in these last-of-the-last days, we are going to need one another more and more. That is why the apostle Paul said, "As we have therefore opportunity, let us do good unto all men, especially unto them who are of the household of faith" (Galatians 6:10).

The word "especially" here is the Greek word *malista*, which means *especially, particularly*, or *most of all*. God wants us to pay particular attention to those who are of "the household of faith." In Greek, the word "household" is *oikeious*, and it describes *one's own house* or *a domestic unit that is closely linked*. It can also denote *those who adhere to or belong to the same group* or *those who have a kindred spirit*.

Have you ever really stopped to think about who you're linked with? Who are you doing life with that shares a kindred spirit? What family of faith do you belong to? If you don't have one, you need to prayerfully find one. You cannot sail safely through these turbulent times alone.

We're Called To 'Provoke and Exhort' Each Other To Do What's Right

The principle of doing life together is seen throughout God's Word. Take for example what the writer of Hebrews said in Hebrews 10:24:

And let us consider one another to provoke unto love and to good works.

The word "consider" here is the Greek word *katanoeo*, which is a compound of the word *kata*, meaning *down*, and the word *noeo*, meaning *to think*. When these words are joined to form *katanoeo*, it means *to thoroughly consider, to think something through from the top to the bottom*, or *to deeply ponder*. It pictures a person engaged in focused and concentrated consideration. Moreover, it is the idea of *mulling something over, carefully contemplating a matter*, or *pondering and carefully looking at a particular issue*. In other words, God is calling us to examine, contemplate, and fully study how we can provoke each other to love and good works.

In Greek, the word "provoke" is *paroxusmos*, and it describes *the prodding and impelling of a person to do something*. It can even mean *to call into combat*. In these last days, we are dealing with many difficulties, and at times we're tempted to withdraw from everyone and everything and not do anything. Have you been there and done that? That's why we need each other — to provoke each other to right action and to take a stand on God's Word and against the enemy.

Hebrews 10:25 then adds:

> **Not forsaking the assembling of ourselves together, as the manner of some is; but exhorting one another: and so much the more, as ye see the day approaching.**

The word "exhorting" in this verse is very important. It is the remarkable Greek word *parakaleo*, a compound of *para* and *kaleo*. The preposition *para* means *alongside*, and *kaleo* means *I call*. When compounded, the word *parakaleo* means *to draw alongside someone else to appeal or to call out to them* or *to encourage and exhort*. It carries the idea of *consoling someone else* or *igniting someone to action by appealing to them*. Interestingly, this word *parakaleo* was used by the military to denote a commander who charged and exhorted troops to face battles bravely and to fight to victory.

In these last days, when we're surrounded by a sea of destructive waters and raging waves, we need like-minded believers with a kindred spirit in our lives who will regularly encourage us to hold our head high, throw our shoulders back, and bravely move forward in the face of challenges.

There's Exponential Power in Working Together

Solomon, one of the wisest men to ever live, knew the indispensable strength of doing life with others. He wrote about it in the book of Ecclesiastes, saying:

> **Two are better than one; because they have a good reward for their labour.**
>
> **For if they fall, the one will lift up his fellow: but woe to him that is alone when he falleth; for he hath not another to help him up.**
>
> **— Ecclesiastes 4:9,10**

Two people working together on something can accomplish so much more than one alone. Rather than achieving double for their work, what they produce together is exponentially greater. And if either one falls or gets hurt, the other is there to help pick him or her up. If someone is alone and falls, there is no one there to help.

The Bible goes on to say:

> **Again, if two lie together, then they have heat: but how can one be warm alone?**
>
> **And if one prevail against him, two shall withstand him; and a threefold cord is not quickly broken.**
> — Ecclesiastes 4:11,12

Friend, it's always better to be a part of a team or a family of faith. Noah couldn't do the monumental task of building the Ark and caring for all the animals by himself, which is why God called Noah *and his family* — they were a family of faith. Once the floodwaters receded, everyone exited the Ark *together* and they worked to replenish the earth *together*.

And just as Noah couldn't do it alone, neither can you. You need a family of faith to belong to. This includes a healthy local church as well as good friends who will stand by you through the good and bad and always be willing to speak the truth to you in love (*see* Ephesians 4:15). If you're still looking for a good local church to call home, call us! We'd love to be a part of your family of faith. We'll pray with you and walk with you through life's challenges.

Questions and Answers With Rick Renner

In the program, Rick answered the following question from one of our viewers.

Q. What does the word 'sorcery' mean?

A. The word "sorcery" appears in several places throughout the New Testament. It is the Greek word *pharmakeia*, which is the term for *medicines or drugs that inhibit a person's personality or change his behavior*. Today, we would call these *mind-altering drugs*. The word *pharmakeia* is where we get the words "pharmacy" and "pharmaceutical drugs."

Interestingly, when you read Revelation 9:21, the Bible prophesies that at the very end of the age, the world will become an overmedicated place and will not turn away from (repent of) their use of drugs. Now, if you need medication, by all means, take medication. But what the Bible is talking about at the very end of the age is an addiction to drugs (*pharmakeia*, translated as "sorcery") as a means of escaping reality instead of seeking the real, lasting solution to their problems, which is the person of Jesus Christ.

How many people do you know today who are overmedicated? This is happening in society just as the Bible predicted it would. But with the power of the Holy Spirit and a steady diet of God's Word, you can gain and maintain freedom from substance addictions and stay filled with the Holy Spirit, who is the real answer you need.

In our next lesson, we'll learn how to hear God's personal instructions for you!

STUDY QUESTIONS

> **Study to shew thyself approved unto God, a workman that needeth not to be ashamed, rightly dividing the word of truth.**
> **— 2 Timothy 2:15**

1. When you read Ecclesiastes 4:9-12, who comes to mind in Scripture? In Ruth 1:16 and 17 and First Samuel 18:1-4 and 20:34-42, who were the faithful friends that stuck by each other when things became increasingly difficult?
2. Oftentimes our *team* is our biological family, but sometimes our team consists of other people God has placed in our lives to help us. We see this demonstrated in Luke 5:17-26, with a man whom Jesus ministered to. How did this man's team literally change his entire life? What does this say to you personally about being involved in other people's lives?
3. When we look around at today's world and consider the widespread use of substances to cope with the challenges of everyday life, we can easily begin to wonder, *What if they could help me feel better? Is it really worth it to stay away from these things?* If that has crossed your mind, look at Proverbs 20:1 and Proverbs 23:20-22,29-35. What does life look like when you dive deep into substances to cope?

PRACTICAL APPLICATION

> But be ye doers of the word, and not hearers only, deceiving your own selves.
> —James 1:22

1. Noah's tight-knit group was made up of his wife, his sons, and his sons' wives. These were "his people." Do you know who "your people" are? Who has God divinely connected you with to share in the work He's asked you to do?
2. How do the people on "your team" encourage you most? How are you effectively encouraging *them* to keep doing good and pursuing Jesus without growing weary?
3. Have you ever tried to take care of a huge task by yourself? What was it? How much better and faster do you think your experience would have been if you'd had a team to help you?
4. Take a minute to pray and ask the Holy Spirit to show you who your team is and whose team you need to be on as you move forward.

LESSON 5

TOPIC
Getting God's Personal Instructions for You!

SCRIPTURES
1. **Matthew 24:37** — But as the days of Noe [Noah] were, so shall also the coming of the Son of man be.
2. **Genesis 7:16,17** — And they that went in, went in male and female of all flesh, as God had commanded him: and the Lord shut him in. And the flood was forty days upon the earth; and the waters increased, and bare up the ark, and it was lift up above the earth.
3. **Genesis 6:11-22** — The earth also was corrupt before God, and the earth was filled with violence. And God looked upon the earth, and, behold, it was corrupt; for all flesh had corrupted his way upon the earth. And God said unto Noah, The end of all flesh is come before

me; for the earth is filled with violence through them; and, behold, I will destroy them with the earth. Make thee an ark of gopher wood; rooms shalt thou make in the ark, and shalt pitch it within and without with pitch. And this is the fashion which thou shalt make it of: The length of the ark shall be three hundred cubits, the breadth of it fifty cubits, and the height of it thirty cubits. A window shalt thou make to the ark, and in a cubit shalt thou finish it above; and the door of the ark shalt thou set in the side thereof; with lower, second, and third stories shalt thou make it. And, behold, I, even I, do bring a flood of waters upon the earth, to destroy all flesh, wherein is the breath of life, from under heaven; and every thing that is in the earth shall die. But with thee will I establish my covenant; and thou shalt come into the ark, thou, and thy sons, and thy wife, and thy sons' wives with thee. And of every living thing of all flesh, two of every sort shalt thou bring into the ark, to keep them alive with thee; they shall be male and female. Of fowls after their kind, and of cattle after their kind, of every creeping thing of the earth after his kind, two of every sort shall come unto thee, to keep them alive. And take thou unto thee of all food that is eaten, and thou shalt gather it to thee; and it shall be for food for thee, and for them. Thus did Noah; according to all that God commanded him, so did he.

4. **Hebrews 11:7** — By faith Noah, being warned of God of things not seen as yet, moved with fear, prepared an ark to the saving of his house by the which he condemned the world, and became heir of the righteousness which is by faith.

GREEK WORDS

1. "being warned" — χρηματίζω (*chrematidzo*): a business transaction; to advise or consult with one about important affairs; in this case, to be advised and consulted with by God: literally, being divinely advised, consulted, and warned
2. "not seen as yet" — μηδέπω (*medepo*): not yet or not ever before
3. "moved with fear" — εὐλαβέομαι (*eulabeomai*): to take action urgently and seriously

SYNOPSIS

Many researchers and explorers have had the mistaken idea that Noah's Ark is at the top of Mount Ararat. But that is impossible, because modern-day Mount Ararat is a stratovolcano consisting of both a lower and higher peak, which has erupted several times in the thousands of years since the Flood. If the Ark had landed there, it would have been destroyed by volcanic activity — not to mention, the height and size of the mountain would not be the same as it is today.

As we've noted, Scripture reveals that the Ark came to rest "…upon the mountains of Ararat" (Genesis 8:4). The fact is, Ararat is an extensive mountain range that spans hundreds of square miles. And it's in the lower Ararat mountains of eastern Turkey — right on the border of Iran and Armenia — that the massive, ship-shaped formation is located. Specifically, the Ark's remnants are situated on a lower mountain called Judi, and because the dimensions of the vessel found there fit the Genesis 6 account, many archeologists and scientists now affirm that this man-made formation is indeed Noah's Ark. Although the structure has collapsed and is mud-encased after thousands of years of weathering, ERT scans and ground-penetrating radar confirm the ship had three levels, multiple rooms, and was about 515 feet in length — exactly as God had instructed Noah to build it.

To be clear: Noah didn't just sit down one day and decide to build an Ark. God gave him clear, detailed instructions regarding the construction of the Ark and the animals he was supposed to take with him. Step by step, Noah and his family diligently followed the instructions he received, which is exactly what we need to do to survive the destruction and whirlwind of wickedness in the world in these last days.

The emphasis of this lesson:

If you're going to sail through this end-time season in victory, you need to hear and heed God's specific instructions for you. If you'll open your ears and listen, God will speak to you and direct you through His Word, His Holy Spirit, and His people in the Church.

What We Know So Far

Looking once more at our anchor verses, the Bible says that after Noah and his family finished building the Ark, "they that went in, went in male and female of all flesh, as God had commanded him: and the Lord shut him in. And the flood was forty days upon the earth; and the waters increased, and bare up the ark, and it was lift up above the earth" (Genesis 7:16,17). This tells us that the same waters that annihilated everything on earth elevated Noah and his family. Higher and higher they rose until they literally floated on the sea of destruction, which is exactly what God wants us to do in these last days.

In our first lesson, we saw that when we repent of our sins and invite Jesus to be our Lord and Savior, God tucks us away deeply inside Christ, our Ark of safety. In Lesson 2, we learned how the Word of God functions like the drogue stones that hung from the sides of the Ark. When the Word is anchoring our life, we remain stable and steady even through turbulent times. In our third lesson, we discovered the importance of living a life of sacrifice and how it opens the door to God's presence, His power, and His promises. And in Lesson 4, we learned the need to have our own tight-knit group to work with as we go through difficult times.

What else is needed in order to sail through these turbulent times victoriously? Like Noah, we need to have very clear instructions from the Lord. Some people might ask the question, "Do you really believe God is still speaking to people today?" And the answer is, *absolutely*! Just as God spoke to people in the Old Testament times, He is still speaking to people today — and even more so. Why? Because we have the Holy Spirit living inside us! We are literally the "temple of the Holy Spirit" (*see* 1 Corinthians 3:16; 6:19). Jesus said, "When the Spirit of truth comes, he will guide you into all truth. He will not speak on his own but will tell you what he has heard. He will tell you about the future" (John 16:13 *NLT*). If we'll regularly seek God and open our ears to listen, the Holy Spirit will give us the instructions we need to walk every step of the way through this end-time age.

Rampant Violence and Corruption Were the Cause for the Global Cleansing

According to the genealogies recorded in Genesis, Noah is the tenth generation from Adam, and during his lifetime, the condition of society was absolutely deplorable. God confirms this in His Word, which says:

> **The earth also was corrupt before God, and the earth was filled with violence.**
>
> **And God looked upon the earth, and, behold, it was corrupt; for all flesh had corrupted his way upon the earth.**

> **And God said unto Noah, The end of all flesh is come before me; for the earth is filled with violence through them; and, behold, I will destroy them with the earth.**
> — **Genesis 6:11-13**

Notice that verse 13 begins with the words, "And God said unto Noah…." This is where God began to give Noah the instructions he and his family would need to survive the catastrophe that was about to destroy the earth. First, God said, "Make thee an ark of gopher wood; rooms shalt thou make in the ark, and shalt pitch it within and without with pitch" (Genesis 6:14). Now, we don't know what gopher wood was, and it likely didn't exist until that time. It appears to have been some kind of laminated wood that was very durable, and that is what God told Noah to use.

The Ark's Dimensions Were Very Specific

God's instructions continue in verse 15 where He told Noah:

> **And this is the fashion which thou shalt make it of: The length of the ark shall be three hundred cubits, the breadth of it fifty cubits, and the height of it thirty cubits.**
> — **Genesis 6:15**

Here we see that God instructed Noah to make the Ark 300 cubits long by 50 cubits wide by 30 cubits high. This brings up the question, *what was the length of a cubit?* You may have heard that a Hebrew cubit was 18 inches long, but did Noah use the Hebrew cubit measurement? Probably not, since it was not in existence at the time of Noah, because Eber — Noah's great, great grandson and father of the Hebrews — had not yet been born.

Keep in mind that Moses penned the narrative of the Ark's construction. He had been schooled in Egypt's finest institutions, making it much more likely that the cubit referred to in Genesis 6:15 is the **Egyptian cubit**, which was approximately **20.6 inches**. If we plug this measurement into the dimensions God gave Noah, this is what we come up with:

Length: 300 cubits X 20.6 inches = 6,180 inches or approximately **515 feet long**

Width: 50 cubits X 20.6 inches = 1,030 inches or approximately **85 feet wide**

Height: 30 cubits X 20.6 inches = 618 inches or approximately **50 feet high**

Thus, the Ark was approximately **515 feet long by 85 feet wide by 50 feet high**. And remember, God had instructed Noah to make "rooms" inside the Ark (*see* Genesis 6:14). What other specific instructions did Noah receive regarding the Ark? Look at verse 16:

> **A window shalt thou make to the ark, and in a cubit shalt thou finish it above; and the door of the ark shalt thou set in the side thereof; with lower, second, and third stories shalt thou make it.**
> **— Genesis 6:16**

Here we see that God told Noah to include a window, which was to be about 20.6 inches high (1 cubit), as well as a single door in the Ark's side. God also specified that the Ark was to have three stories. The purpose in citing these details is because if the Ark was found today, it would need to meet these biblical criteria — and that is what the ship-shaped remains on Mount Judi do. Ground-penetrating radar confirms that the massive formation encased in mud has three levels and multiple rooms — exactly like we read in verses 14 and 16.

God Prophesied to Noah What Was About To Happen

At this point in God's conversation with Noah, He moved into prophetic mode and began to give Noah a "big picture" — an overview of what was going to take place.

> **And, behold, I, even I, do bring a flood of waters upon the earth, to destroy all flesh, wherein is the breath of life, from under heaven; and every thing that is in the earth shall die.**
>
> **But with thee will I establish my covenant; and thou shalt come into the ark, thou, and thy sons, and thy wife, and thy sons' wives with thee.**
> **— Genesis 6:17,18**

God told Noah that He was going to bring floodwaters on the earth, and those waters were going to destroy all flesh and everything living on the earth. Imagine the weight of those words hitting Noah's ears and sinking into his mind. *Wow!* Everything was about to be wiped out — everything except Noah and his wife and his sons and their wives.

Jesus prophesied, "But as the days of Noe [Noah] were, so shall also the coming of the Son of man be" (Matthew 24:37). This tells us that just as there were many bizarre activities taking place on earth before the Flood, similar things will take place again before Christ returns. In fact, we are seeing many activities from Noah's day replicated in our day. But as bizarre as things may seem, they are likely to become even more bizarre.

Noah Also Received Instructions Regarding the Animals and Food

The plan to take a sampling of all the animals onto the Ark was not Noah's idea — it was God's. In His infinite wisdom and foresight, He instructed Noah:

> **And of every living thing of all flesh, two of every sort shalt thou bring into the ark, to keep them alive with thee; they shall be male and female.**
>
> **Of fowls after their kind, and of cattle after their kind, of every creeping thing of the earth after his kind, two of every sort shall come unto thee, to keep them alive.**
> **— Genesis 6:19,20**

Isn't that interesting? There are only two genders of each kind of animal — a male and a female. It's the same with human beings: "God created man in his own image, in the image of God created he him; *male* and *female* created he them" (Genesis 1::27). It takes a male and a female to create offspring of the same kind and ensure the survival of that species.

God also gave Noah instructions concerning the gathering of food for the voyage. He said:

> **And take thou unto thee of all food that is eaten, and thou shalt gather it to thee; and it shall be for food for thee, and for them.**
> **— Genesis 6:21**

So from Genesis 6:13 to Genesis 6:21, God downloaded very specific instructions to Noah regarding the building of the Ark and the gathering of the animals to preserve both human and animal life through the cataclysmic flood that He was bringing on the earth. How did Noah respond to the Lord's instructions? Genesis 6:22 says, "Thus did Noah; according to all that God commanded him, so did he."

Note that Scripture says God *commanded* Noah. He didn't just say, "This flood is going to be a real tough situation, Noah, so I want you to go ahead and build a boat of some kind to save you and your family — and you should probably take some animals with you too. Do what you think is best…I'm sure you'll figure it out." Wouldn't that have been ridiculous?

God gave Noah very clear instructions, and as you seek Him and open your spiritual ears to hear what He's saying, He promises to "instruct you and teach you in the way you should go" (Psalm 32:8 *NIV*). This verse continues, "[He] will counsel you with [His] loving eye on you."

God Divinely Warned and Advised Noah

There is another mention of Noah in the book of Hebrews. Here, the Holy Spirit highlights "By faith Noah, being warned of God of things not seen as yet, moved with fear, prepared an ark to the saving of his house by the which he condemned the world, and became heir of the righteousness which is by faith" (Hebrews 11:7).

The phrase "being warned" in this verse is a translation of the Greek word *chrematidzo*, which is a term that describes *a business transaction*. It means *to advise or consult with one about important affairs*, which is a description of the kind of relationship Noah had with God. In this case, Noah was advised and consulted by God about what was coming and how to deal with it. Thus, the word *chrematidzo* literally denotes *being divinely advised, consulted, and warned*. God cared so much about Noah and his family and the survival of the animals that He divinely warned him of what was coming and advised him on exactly how to deal with it.

According to Hebrews 11:7, the things that were coming on the world were "not seen as yet." This phrase is a translation of the Greek word *medepo*, which means *not yet* or *not ever before*. Imagine what it must have been like for Noah to receive a foretelling of events that were going to happen, and he had no frame of reference with which to understand it. The coming rain, the springs of the deep bursting, and the earth being totally covered by floodwaters were something that had never happened.

In the same way, for those of us living right now at the very end of the age, some things are coming on the earth that have never happened before, and we need God's divine counsel and advice as to how we are to prepare for and handle it. Like Noah, we too must be moved with a reverential, godly fear to hear and obey what the Lord is saying.

Noah Took God Seriously and Acted With Urgency

The phrase "moved with fear" in Hebrews 11:7 is the Greek word *eulabeomai*, which means *to take action urgently and seriously*. That is how Noah responded to God's warning and instructions. Did you ever stop to think what would have happened had Noah said, "That's very interesting, God, and I appreciate You talking to me about it. But what You're asking me to do is too much, and I'm just not willing to take it on right now." If Noah had responded like that, he, his family, and the entire human race would have ceased to exist.

Friend, we need to learn a lesson from Noah and take what God says seriously and then urgently respond. Because he walked closely with God (*see* Genesis 6:9), He was able to hear God's voice. He then took God's warning seriously and obediently carried out His instructions (*see* Genesis 6:22; 7:5). As a result of Noah's obedience, his entire household — and the animal kingdom — was saved. Amazingly, the population of the earth was restarted through this one family.

For you and your family to sail through this end-time season, you need God's instructions for your life. God will speak to you very clearly — first from His Word, second by His Holy Spirit, and third through His people, such as pastors and ministers, as well as fellow believers in the Church. So stay in God's Word, reading and studying it. Spend time regularly in His presence, talking with and listening to the Holy Spirit. And continue to stay connected with a healthy local church.

As God speaks to you and makes His instructions clear, it is your job to obey what He says. If you follow His direction, you will make it through any season you're facing, regardless of how turbulent the times seem to be.

Questions and Answers With Rick Renner

In the program, Rick answered the following question from one of our viewers.

Q. What's the greatest enemy you've faced?

A. "Well, I've faced many enemies in my life," Rick responded. "I write about several of them in my book *Unlikely*. But I have learned the greatest enemy I've ever faced is not the devil or anyone else — it's me.

"The Bible tells us in Proverbs 16:32 that he who rules or controls his own spirit is mightier than one who conquers a city. God has taught me that if I can master *me*, there's nothing I can't do. The devil is not a problem, and there's no mountain that I cannot climb if I learn to receive the power of the Holy Spirit and operate in self-control. That is what I mean by 'mastering me.'

"This is a daily choice to crucify my flesh and yield to the promptings and power of the Holy Spirit. Like the apostle Paul, I've learned to say each day, 'I have been crucified with Christ and I no longer live, but Christ lives in me. The life I now live in the body, I live by faith in the Son of God, who loved me and gave himself for me' (Galatians 2:20 *NIV*). This is what it means to present myself to the Lord and be a 'living sacrifice' that is holy and pleasing to Him. This is how I've learned to 'master me,' and it's how you can learn to *master you!*"

In our next lesson, we will examine the meaning of Jesus' recurring statement: "He who has ears to hear, let him hear what the Spirit is saying."

STUDY QUESTIONS

Study to shew thyself approved unto God, a workman that needeth not to be ashamed, rightly dividing the word of truth.
— 2 Timothy 2:15

1. What did you think when you found out that the Ark wasn't actually on top of modern-day Mount Ararat, but on Mount Judi, a lower mountain in the Ararat range? How valuable do you think it is to study both Scripture and archaeological evidence together, instead of only focusing on one or the other?
2. Can you imagine living on a planet where literally everyone's tendencies were evil, ALL the time? That's how it was in Noah's day. When you look around at our world, how far do you think we are from reaching that level of corruption?
3. Whether you've already received specific instructions from God or not, the need to receive them will come up over and over again

throughout your life. According to Proverbs 3:5-8; John 16:13; and Isaiah 30:21, what does He promise to do for you as you seek Him?

PRACTICAL APPLICATION

> But be ye doers of the word, and not hearers only, deceiving your own selves.
> —James 1:22

1. After going through this lesson, what stands out to you about the value of having specific directions from God before you begin a long-term project or pursue a large goal?
2. Do you feel in your heart that God's given you specific directions on what to do in your career, relationships, or ministry? If so, write out what He's shown you. If not, invite Him to show you what you need to see and to tell you what you need to know at this time.
3. As you read through the very specific instructions God gave Noah for the Ark, how different do you think the Ark would have been had he not had such detailed directions? If God had just given general instructions like, "Build a boat and I'll send some animals," do you think everyone and everything would have survived?

LESSON 6

TOPIC

Do You Have Ears To Hear What the Spirit Is Saying?

SCRIPTURES

1. **Matthew 24:37** — But as the days of Noe [Noah] were, so shall also the coming of the Son of man be.
2. **Genesis 7:16,17** — And they that went in, went in male and female of all flesh, as God had commanded him: and the Lord shut him in. And the flood was forty days upon the earth; and the waters increased, and bare up the ark, and it was lift up above the earth.

3. **Hebrews 11:7** — By faith Noah, being warned of God of things not seen as yet, moved with fear, prepared an ark to the saving of his house by the which he condemned the world, and became heir of the righteousness which is by faith.
4. **Genesis 6:13-17** — And God said unto Noah, The end of all flesh is come before me; for the earth is filled with violence through them; and, behold, I will destroy them with the earth. Make thee an ark of gopher wood; rooms shalt thou make in the ark, and shalt pitch it within and without with pitch. And this is the fashion which thou shalt make it of: The length of the ark shall be three hundred cubits, the breadth of it fifty cubits, and the height of it thirty cubits. A window shalt thou make to the ark, and in a cubit shalt thou finish it above; and the door of the ark shalt thou set in the side thereof; with lower, second, and third stories shalt thou make it. And, behold, I, even I, do bring a flood of waters upon the earth, to destroy all flesh, wherein is the breath of life, from under heaven; and every thing that is in the earth shall die.
5. **Genesis 6:22** — Thus did Noah; according to all that God commanded him, so did he.
6. **Genesis 7:1** — And the Lord said unto Noah, Come thou and all thy house into the ark; for thee have I seen righteous before me in this generation.
7. **Matthew 11:15** — He that hath ears to hear, let him hear.
8. **Matthew 13:9** — Who hath ears to hear, let him hear.
9. **Matthew 13:43** — …Who hath ears to hear, let him hear.
10. **Mark 4:9** — And he said unto them, He that hath ears to hear, let him hear.
11. **Mark 4:23** — If any man have ears to hear, let him hear.
12. **Luke 8:8** — …And when he had said these things, he cried, He that hath ears to hear, let him hear.
13. **Revelation 2:7** — He that hath an ear, let him hear what the Spirit saith unto the churches.…
14. **Revelation 2:11** — He that hath an ear, let him hear what the Spirit saith unto the churches.…
15. **Revelation 2:17** — He that hath an ear, let him hear what the Spirit saith unto the churches.…

16. **Revelation 2:29** — He that hath an ear, let him hear what the Spirit saith unto the churches.
17. **Revelation 3:6** — He that hath an ear, let him hear what the Spirit saith unto the churches.
18. **Revelation 3:13** — He that hath an ear, let him hear what the Spirit saith unto the churches.
19. **Revelation 3:22** — He that hath an ear, let him hear what the Spirit saith unto the churches.

GREEK WORDS

1. "being warned" — **χρηματίζω** (*chrematidzo*): a business transaction; to advise or consult with one about important affairs; in this case, to be advised and consulted with by God: literally, being divinely advised, consulted, and warned
2. "not seen as yet" — **μηδέπω** (*medepo*): not yet or not ever before
3. "moved with fear" — **εὐλαβέομαι** (*eulabeomai*): to take action urgently and seriously
4. "prepared" — **κατασκευάζω** (*kataskeuadzo*): he put forth effort to build a vessel
5. "to the saving of his house" — for the explicit purpose of saving his own household

SYNOPSIS

The things that we're seeing happening in society today were forecasted by Jesus Himself during His life nearly 2,000 years ago. He said, "But as the days of Noe [Noah] were, so shall also the coming of the Son of man be" (Matthew 24:37). Because of the widespread evil and corruption in Noah's day, God brought a global flood on the earth to cleanse it. But before the Flood came, God told Noah what was about to happen and gave him explicit instructions on how to save himself and his family.

In these last days, God wants to instruct you and your family on what you need to do to thrive and sail victoriously through to the end of the age. He is speaking to His people all the time, but to hear the instructions He's giving, *you have to have ears that hear what He is saying.* When you open your spiritual ears and ask God to direct you concerning your family, your finances, your future, and everything else, He will speak to you by His Spirit and show you what to do.

The emphasis of this lesson:

Noah came from a long line of people who had ears to hear what God was saying. God is always speaking, and if we'll open our spiritual ears to listen and hear His voice, we will receive His divine instructions for every situation we face in life.

A Review of Lessons 1-5

Without question, we are facing some very turbulent, end-time conditions in the world. It seems as if society at large has gone crazy in its thinking — calling what's wrong right and what's right wrong. Thankfully, we can keep our head on straight by opening our spiritual ears and learning to listen to the voice of God through His Holy Spirit.

That's what Noah did. The Bible says, "…Noah walked [in habitual fellowship] with God" (Genesis 6:9 *AMPC*), and in that ongoing close fellowship, God warned him of the coming flood and instructed him to build an ark that would preserve him, his family, and a sampling of all the animals. After nearly 100 years of construction, the Ark was finished, "And they that went in, went in male and female of all flesh, as God had commanded him: and the Lord shut him in. And the flood was forty days upon the earth; and the waters increased, and bare up the ark, and it was lift up above the earth" (Genesis 7:16,17).

As the waters increased and the entire earth was engulfed by the Flood, absolutely everything was destroyed — except Noah, his family, and the animals that were on the Ark. Because they had received God's instructions and obeyed, they were literally lifted above and floated on the same waters that destroyed everything else.

Here is a brief recap of what we've learned in our first five lessons:

Lesson 1: We need to be sealed tight in Jesus Christ — God's *ark of safety*.

Lesson 2: We must have God's Word anchored in our life to stay stable and steady in these turbulent times.

Lesson 3: Making sacrifices to God brings His presence, His power, and His promises into our lives and keeps us afloat in these last days.

Lesson 4: We need to know who "our people" are and work together with them to accomplish the assignment God has given us.

Lesson 5: Each of us needs to receive God's personal instructions for our life.

And in **Lesson 6**, we are going to focus on the need to have ears to hear what the Holy Spirit is saying.

Noah Was Divinely Advised and Warned by God Himself

As we saw in our last lesson, the book of Hebrews also makes mention of Noah. Specifically, it says, "By faith Noah, being warned of God of things not seen as yet, moved with fear, prepared an ark to the saving of his house by the which he condemned the world, and became heir of the righteousness which is by faith" (Hebrews 11:7).

The words "being warned" in Greek is the word *chrematidzo*, which is a term that describes *a business transaction*. Its use here tells us that Noah had a businesslike relationship with God in which God was the boss and Noah did what he was told. This word *chrematidzo* means *to advise or consult with one about important affairs*, and in this case, it means Noah was being *divinely advised, consulted, and warned* by God "of things not yet seen."

Since God was the boss and Noah was the servant, he did whatever God told him to do, and because Noah's ears were opened, he was literally being divinely advised, consulted, and warned by God Himself.

Listening to and Hearing God's Instructions Was a Practice for Generations in Noah's Family

If you look at Noah's ancestors, you will see that they, too, were listening to God's instructions and hearing from Him. In fact, for several generations, God had been speaking to Noah's entire family, and they were prophetically "in the know" about what He was going to do.

For example, Noah's great-great-grandfather was *Jared*, and Jared's name means *shall come down*. This is significant because rabbinical history tells us that it was during the days of Jared that fallen angels began to come down to comingle with earthly women, and through their illicit sexual relations, giants were born. This bizarre intermixing between the celestial beings and human women produced hybrids that were the "mighty men of renown" talked about in Genesis 6:4.

When Jared was 162 years old, he fathered a son named *Enoch*, who was the great-grandfather of Noah. Enoch's name means *to teach* or *to correct*. Of all of Noah's ancestors, it seems Enoch heard from God most clearly. In fact, he heard from God so explicitly that he made a written record of what the Lord revealed to him. These ancient documents are what became known as the *Book of Enoch*. These writings were well-known by Jesus, the apostles, and the people of their time. Jude, the half-brother of Jesus, actually quotes Enoch's prophecy concerning the Second Coming of Christ at the very end of the age (*see* Jude 14,15).

Genesis 5:24 tells us that Enoch walked so closely with God that one day God just took him to Heaven without experiencing death. But before Enoch was raptured, he fathered many sons and daughters, including a son named *Methuselah*. Interestingly, the name Methuselah means *his death shall bring* or *when he dies, it will come*. Thus, Methuselah and his family knew that when he died, it would signal that the judgment of God was coming.

The Bible says when Methuselah was 187, he had a son whose name was *Lamech* (*see* Genesis 5:25), and the name Lamech means *lamentation* or *sorrow*. The reason he was so named is because, at the time of his birth, the world was filled with much sorrow and grief. When Lamech was 182, he became the father of *Noah*, whose name means *comfort* or *rest*.

Noah's birth was a prophetic statement to the world that during his life, *comfort* and *rest* would finally come to the planet. The violence and corruption resulting from the fallen angels and the birth of the giants would be ended, and humanity would be given a fresh, new start. The point of going through Noah's lineage is to help you understand that Noah wasn't the only one hearing from God — he came from an entire family of people who heard from God and obeyed His instructions.

Each generation received divine revelation and then passed it on to the next, which shows us that we need to have ears that hear the Spirit of God first. It also demonstrates the vital need to pass on to our children and our grandchildren the truth of God's Word and to teach them how to hear His voice.

[To help you fine-tune your ears to hear God's instructions for your life, we encourage you to obtain Rick's series *Knowing the Will of God*, which you can find at **renner.org**.]

What God Told Noah To Do Was Unprecedented

Looking once more at Hebrews 11:7, it says, "By faith Noah, being warned of God of things not seen as yet, moved with fear, prepared an ark to the saving of his house…." In Greek, the words "not seen as yet" are a translation of the word *medepo*, which means *not yet* or *not ever before*. Hence, God was warning and advising Noah about things no one in the world had ever seen.

Think about it: When God advised and warned Noah about a worldwide flood, no one had ever seen anything of this magnitude. Before the Flood, all vegetation was watered by a mist that came up from the ground (*see* Genesis 2:5,6). Furthermore, the instruction to build the Ark was also something he and everyone else had never witnessed.

The same can be said of God's instruction to collect two of every kind of animal — a male and a female — and bring them into the Ark, not to mention the direction to gather food for the animals and his family. All these unprecedented tasks were assigned to Noah and his family members and required tremendous resources, time, and labor to execute.

'Moved With Fear,' Noah 'Prepared an Ark to the Saving of His Family'

Nevertheless, when Noah heard God's commands, he was "moved with fear" (*see* Hebrews 11:7). This phrase is a translation of the Greek word *eulabeomai*, which means *to take action urgently and seriously*. Noah knew that he had heard from God, and he was quick to obey. He had a sense of awe and responsibility to do as he had been instructed. Therefore, he "…prepared an ark to the saving of his house…" (Hebrews 11:7).

The word "prepared" here is the Greek word *kataskeuadzo*, which basically means *he put forth intense effort* to build a vessel. That is, Noah put forth everything he had into the construction of the Ark, building it exactly according to the plan God had given him. And he did it "to the saving of his house," which in Greek means *for the explicit purpose of saving his own household.*

Friend, we need to learn a lesson from Noah and take what God says seriously and respond urgently. As God speaks to us and makes His instructions clear, it is our job to obey what He says. If we follow His direction, we will make it through any season we're facing, regardless of how turbulent the times seem to be.

Noah Had Ears To Hear What God Was Saying

The Scripture clearly reveals two things: God was speaking, and Noah was listening. Genesis 6:13 tells us, "And God said unto Noah, The end of all flesh is come before me; for the earth is filled with violence through them; and, behold, I will destroy them with the earth." God spoke and prophesied what He was about to do, and Noah heard Him.

God continued by giving Noah the "plan of salvation" for him and his family. He said, "Make thee an ark of gopher wood; rooms shalt thou make in the ark, and shalt pitch it within and without with pitch. And this is the fashion which thou shalt make it of: The length of the ark shall be three hundred cubits, the breadth of it fifty cubits, and the height of it thirty cubits" (Genesis 6:14,15). Again, God spoke, and Noah listened.

The Lord then added, "A window shalt thou make to the ark, and in a cubit shalt thou finish it above; and the door of the ark shalt thou set in the side thereof; with lower, second, and third stories shalt thou make it" (Genesis 6:16). If you're counting, the command "thou shalt" or "shall" were given by God seven times and clearly indicate 1) He was giving instructions, and 2) Noah was listening.

Then, for a second time, God spoke and prophesied to Noah what He was about to do, declaring, "And, behold, I, even I, do bring a flood of waters upon the earth, to destroy all flesh, wherein is the breath of life, from under heaven; and every thing that is in the earth shall die" (Genesis 6:17).

What was Noah's response to all these instructions? "Thus did Noah; according to all that God commanded him, so did he" (Genesis 6:22). When the Ark was completed and it was finally time to get on board, "…The Lord said unto Noah, Come thou and all thy house into the ark;

for thee have I seen righteous before me in this generation" (Genesis 7:1). The reason we have a record of all this is because God was speaking, and Noah was listening — he had ears to hear the Lord, and he responded in obedience. Right now, God is speaking, but to hear Him, we need to have spiritual ears to hear what He's saying.

When Jesus Says Something *Thirteen* Times, We Need To Stop and Seriously Take Note of It!

It's no accident the writers of the gospels repeatedly documented Jesus pleading with the people to "have ears to hear" what He was saying. Consider these passages:

- In **Matthew 11:15**, Jesus told the multitudes, "He that hath ears to hear, let him hear."
- In **Matthew 13:9**, Jesus said to the crowd by the sea, "Who hath ears to hear, let him hear."
- In **Matthew 13:43**, Jesus said to His disciples, "…Who hath ears to hear, let him hear."
- In **Mark 4:9**, Jesus told the people on the shore, "…He that hath ears to hear, let him hear."
- In **Mark 4:23**, Jesus said to His disciples, "If any man have ears to hear, let him hear."
- In **Luke 8:8**, after sharing the parable of the sower with a crowd from the surrounding cities, "…[Jesus] cried, He that hath ears to hear, let him hear."

Not only did Jesus repeatedly make this statement in the gospels, but He also said it to each one of the seven churches in the book of Revelation. The apostle John had a front-row seat to see and hear Jesus as He passionately dictated His letters to the pastors and people of these congregations.

- **To the church at Ephesus, Jesus said:**

  "He that hath an ear, let him hear what the Spirit saith unto the churches…" (Revelation 2:7).

- **To the church at Smyrna, Jesus said:**

  "He that hath an ear, let him hear what the Spirit saith unto the churches…" (Revelation 2:11).

- **To the church at Pergamum, Jesus said:**

   "He that hath an ear, let him hear what the Spirit saith unto the churches…" (Revelation 2:17).

- **To the church at Thyatira, Jesus said:**

   "He that hath an ear, let him hear what the Spirit saith unto the churches" (Revelation 2:29).

- **To the church at Sardis, Jesus said:**

   "He that hath an ear, let him hear what the Spirit saith unto the churches" (Revelation 3:6).

- **To the church at Philadelphia, Jesus said:**

   "He that hath an ear, let him hear what the Spirit saith unto the churches" (Revelation 3:13).

- **To the church at Laodicea, Jesus said:**

   "He that hath an ear, let him hear what the Spirit saith unto the churches" (Revelation 3:22).

Friend, God has been — and *still is* — speaking! He is speaking all the time and will give you all the instructions you need to sail through whatever you're facing right now and whatever is up ahead. The question is: *Do you have ears to hear what His Spirit is saying?*

Remember, because Noah had ears to hear what God was saying, he and his family built the Ark, and it was lifted high above the earth and floated on the sea of destruction (*see* Genesis 7:17). If you will listen, God's Word and the Holy Spirit will give you exactly what you need for you and your family to sail through these times in victory.

Questions and Answers With Rick Renner

In the program, Rick answered the following question from one of our viewers.

Q. What Is the RIV?

A. In many of our study guides, you will find a passage of scripture written in the *RIV*. If you've wondered what that is, the letters *RIV* stand for the *Renner Interpretative Version*. Rick is presently working on his own version of the New Testament, and that is what the *RIV* is.

Rick said, "I think you know that I've spent many years studying the Greek New Testament, and I'm crafting my own interpretation, which I call the *Renner Interpretative Version (RIV)*. It's not a translation, but an interpretative version, which means I'm taking all the rich Greek meaning of the words in the New Testament and I'm pulling all the concepts together into a new interpretative version. This will give every reader a fuller understanding of the Greek words in the original text. For those who are hungry and want to dive deeper into the wonderful Word of God, it will be a spiritual feast."

In our next lesson, we will examine the rewards that await those who follow God's instructions.

STUDY QUESTIONS

Study to shew thyself approved unto God, a workman that needeth not to be ashamed, rightly dividing the word of truth.
— 2 Timothy 2:15

1. What new insights did you learn about the generations of Noah's family and their ability to hear from God? What does this show you about the importance of preserving the practice of seeking God and walking closely with Him in your family?
2. When Noah "prepared an ark for the saving of his house," he exerted all the effort he had to accomplish the task. What do Ecclesiastes 9:10 and Colossians 3:23 and 24 say to you about how we should live? Are you living up to this standard?
3. Had you ever viewed God's instructions to Noah to build an ark as His "plan of salvation"? How does this help you better understand the connection between Noah being saved in the Ark and you being saved in Christ? According to Romans 10:9 and 10, what is God's plan of eternal salvation for mankind? (Also consider John 3:15-18,36; 14:6.)

PRACTICAL APPLICATION

But be ye doers of the word, and not hearers only, deceiving your own selves.
— James 1:22

1. The Bible says in Hebrews 11:7 that Noah was "moved with fear," which means he took God's word *seriously* and acted *urgently*. How do *you* usually respond when God asks you to do something? Do you have a nonchalant, "get-to-it-when-I-can" attitude? Or do you take His direction seriously and act in a timely fashion? How can you honor God more in the way you respond to Him?
2. As God speaks to us and makes His instructions clear, it is our job to obey what He says. Can you remember the last thing — big or little — that God asked you to do? If so, what was it, and did you do it? If not, why? If you need to, take a moment to ask God to forgive you for any delay or disobedience, and invite Him to help you do what He's telling you.
3. In at least 13 different places in Scripture, Jesus said, "He who has ears to hear, let him hear." Why do you think He said this so many times? Would you say you have *ears to hear* what the Spirit of God is saying?

LESSON 7

TOPIC

What Happens If You Obey?

SCRIPTURES

1. **Genesis 7:16,17** — And they that went in, went in male and female of all flesh, as God had commanded him: and the Lord shut him in. And the flood was forty days upon the earth; and the waters increased, and bare up the ark, and it was lift up above the earth.
2. **Isaiah 1:19** — If ye be willing and obedient, ye shall eat the good of the land.
3. **Hebrews 11:7** — By faith Noah, being warned of God of things not seen as yet, moved with fear, prepared an ark to the saving of his house....
4. **Genesis 6:13-15** — And God said unto Noah, The end of all flesh is come before me; for the earth is filled with violence through them; and, behold, I will destroy them with the earth. Make thee an ark of gopher wood; rooms shalt thou make in the ark, and shalt pitch it within and without with pitch. And this is the fashion which thou

shalt make it of: The length of the ark shall be three hundred cubits, the breadth of it fifty cubits, and the height of it thirty cubits.
5. **Genesis 6:22** — Thus did Noah; according to all that God commanded him, so did he.
6. **Genesis 7:1** — And the Lord said unto Noah, Come thou and all thy house into the ark; for thee have I seen righteous before me in this generation.
7. **Genesis 7:5** — And Noah did according unto all that the Lord commanded him.

GREEK WORDS

1. "being warned" — χρηματίζω (*chrematidzo*): a business transaction; to advise or consult with one about important affairs; in this case, to be advised and consulted with by God: literally, being divinely advised, consulted, and warned
2. "not seen as yet" — μηδέπω (*medepo*): not yet or not ever before
3. "moved with fear" — εὐλαβέομαι (*eulabeomai*): to take action urgently and seriously
4. "prepared" — κατασκευάζω (*kataskeuadzo*): he put forth effort to build a vessel
5. "ark" — κιβωτός (*kibotos*): a large ship structure constructed of wood; a place designed for warehousing and saving; same word used in Exodus 2:3
6. "to the saving of his house" — for the explicit purpose of saving his own household

SYNOPSIS

The ruins of Noah's Ark, which are lodged within the earth on Mount Judi in the Ararat mountain range, are physical proof of Noah's obedience to what God called him and his family to do. Just imagine if after hearing God's instructions, Noah said, "Lord, I appreciate You letting us know about the coming challenges, but building a huge boat like what You're asking is super expensive and has never been done before. I'm just not willing to invest all that time and money." Or what if Mrs. Noah and her daughters-in-law would have said, "There's no way we're going to get cooped up on a ship with a bunch of smelly animals for God knows how long."

Without the willing obedience of Noah, his wife, his sons, and his sons' wives, they all would have been destroyed with everyone else. The fact is, God knows the future and what is coming in the days ahead, and He knows what actions you need to take to be prepared. If you will have ears to hear what His Spirit is saying and then willingly obey His instructions — even if they don't make sense or feel comfortable — you will rise above and float on the sea of destruction in these last days.

The emphasis of this lesson:

When God instructs us to do something, we must be willing to do it and then follow through with obedience. God gave Noah specific directions, and he took them seriously and acted urgently in obedience. When we're willing and obedient, we will experience the goodness of God.

What If Rick Had Not Obeyed God?

Obedience to what God tells us to do is one of the sweetest-smelling sacrifices we can offer the Lord! If you have children, you understand the indescribable joy that comes when they follow the instructions you've given them. Their willingness to obey is a demonstration of their maturity and love, unlike anything else.

As Rick taught this lesson, he reflected on his own choices and began to ponder what his life and the lives of his wife and children might have been like had they not obeyed what God called them to do. This is what he shared:

> When God first called my family and me to the Former Soviet Union, I was the only one who knew what God had spoken. For some time, I didn't tell anyone because I wasn't so sure I was going to obey. Denise and I had just moved into a beautiful home, and we were really enjoying our life in the United States.
>
> When God spoke, He said, "Hey, it is time for a major course change in your life; I'm going to lead you in another direction. I'm going to relocate you and your family to the former Soviet Union." That was around 1990, and the social and political climate was more like the old Soviet Union at that time. It just wasn't a place I imagined moving to and raising my family and conducting ministry.

Think about it: Who in their right mind would move their family to the Soviet Union? In fact, when God first began calling us there, many people in the Soviet Union were trying to *leave*. I must tell you; it took me quite a while to warm up to the idea. Initially, I internally debated with the Lord and thought, *Am I really going to do what He's telling me to do?*

Then one day I asked Him, "What will happen if I obey You?" And then I just began thinking about what would happen to our ministry, our books, and all our meetings. At that time, everything was growing and thriving. *If I obey You*, I thought, *What's going to happen to all these blessings and the level of success we're experiencing?*

Within moments, I heard the Holy Spirit ask me a question. "And what will you miss if you don't obey Me?" Instantly, my thoughts shifted, and now rather than think about what I was going to be losing, I began to think about what I would be missing if I didn't obey.

Sure, I could not have obeyed the Lord and continued with our ministry as it was, but I would have always wondered what would have happened if I had said *yes*. *What would my wife, my sons, and I have experienced if I had said yes?* I would have had to live with that question for the rest of my life, and that was something I couldn't do.

Therefore, I found myself finally getting into alignment with God and saying *yes* to His instructions. "Lord, I'm going to do what You've asked me to do," I said. And because we obeyed, we have seen the power of God move in the former Soviet Union through our ministry in unimaginable ways. I watched it — and continue to watch it — with my own two eyes. It's extraordinary!

And our children never missed a thing. As a matter of fact, our three sons grew up living in the book of Acts! Rather than just read about it as New Testament history, they have seen and experienced the book of Acts firsthand. Looking back now, I shudder to think about all that we would have missed if my wife, Denise, and I had not said *yes* to God.

We wouldn't have seen the many churches established, the lives of pastors strengthened, and the multitudes of people that have come to the Lord. Likewise, I wouldn't be seated in a chair in a TV studio in Moscow teaching the Word of God to countless people across the globe. And I would still be in the United States saying to myself, *I wonder what would have happened if I had said yes and obeyed God?*

Noah Was Willing *and* Obedient

Noah had an opportunity to say no to God. He likely calculated the cost of constructing the largest ship ever built and the mockery he and his family would have to endure from all those around them. The fact that it took them about 100 years to build the Ark means there were probably a lot of Noah jokes floating around. If Noah and his family had chosen not to obey God, we would not be here today.

But Noah obeyed God, and the Bible says, "And they that went in, went in male and female of all flesh, as God had commanded him: and the Lord shut him in. And the flood was forty days upon the earth; and the waters increased, and bare up the ark, and it was lift up above the earth" (Genesis 7:16,17).

Again, the same waters that destroyed everything else caused Noah and his family to rise higher and higher, and they were lifted above the whole earth. Amazingly, Noah and his family literally floated on the sea of destruction because they obeyed.

In Isaiah 1:19, God declares, "If ye be willing and obedient, ye shall eat the good of the land." To receive this promise, two conditions must be met: you must be *willing* and then you must *obey*. Some people have a *willingness* to do what God is asking, but then they fall short of experiencing His promise because they don't *do* what they've been told. Obedience is our faith in action! If we don't do the God-directed deed, our faith is dead (*see* James 2:14-17). It is being willing *and* obedient that guarantees we will eat the good of the land.

God Warned and Advised Noah of Things 'Not Seen As Yet'

Looking once more at Hebrews 11:7, it says, "By faith Noah, being warned of God of things not seen as yet, moved with fear, prepared an ark to the saving of his house…." The word "faith" here describes *a conviction, a trust, or a faith that is unbendable, unbreakable, unshakable, and unmoving.* By this unbendable, unbreakable faith, Noah knew and understood his God-given assignment.

The words "being warned" — the Greek word *chrematidzo* — describe *a business transaction*, which is a picture of the kind of relationship Noah and God shared. Noah was the servant, and God was the Boss — it was very businesslike. *Chrematidzo* — translated "being warned" — also means *to advise or consult with one about important affairs*. In this case, to be advised and consulted by God. In a literal sense, it depicts *one being divinely advised, consulted, and divinely warned*, and Hebrews 11:7 specifies that Noah was warned "of things not seen as yet."

In Greek, the phrase "not seen as yet" is the word *medepo*, and it describes *things not yet or not ever before*. When God advised, consulted, and warned Noah about a world-wide flood, no one had ever heard of such a thing. Prior to the Flood, we're told in Genesis 2:5 and 6 that no rain had fallen on the earth, but a mist would come up from the ground and water the vegetation.

Hence, rain was an unknown concept in Noah's day, much less a flood caused by the windows of Heaven being opened and underground water caverns bursting forth. No one had ever seen or heard of such a phenomenon — including Noah. Yet, he was hearing this from God, and he was also being instructed by God to build an ark that was going to take 100 years to complete — a task that would require a tremendous amount of resources and effort to accomplish.

Then there was the job of gathering two animals of every kind — male and female — and collecting enough food for them and for Noah and his family. From our vantage point, we know they were on the Ark for just over a year, but they had no idea how long their voyage would last. To accept and carry out these unprecedented tasks was a huge feat of faith. Noah and his family could have said *no*, but instead, they said *yes*, and the rest is history.

'Moved With Fear' Noah 'Prepared an Ark'

Again, Noah received God's divine warnings and counsel and acted in faith. Scripture says "…Moved with fear, [he] prepared an ark to the saving of his house…" (Hebrews 11:7). The words "moved with fear" are a translation of the Greek word *eulabeomai*, which means *to take action urgently and seriously*.

To be clear, Noah knew that he had heard from God, and he was quick to obey. He was not afraid *for* himself or scared *of* God. "Moved with fear" simply means he had a sense of awe and responsibility to do as he had been instructed by God. It was a very important task, and Noah had a sense of urgency that caused him to move forward quickly.

With all his energy and efforts, he "prepared an ark." This word "prepared" in Greek is *kataskeuadzo*, which is a compound of two words: the word *kata*, which means *down* and carries the idea of *intensity*; and the word *skeuadzo*, which means *to build*. When these words are joined together, it doesn't just depict building — it denotes *putting intensity into constructing something*. It means that Noah put forth everything he had into the construction of the Ark — he built it exactly according to the plan God had given him.

Additionally, the Greek word for "ark" is *kibotos*, which describes *a large ship structure constructed of wood* or *a place designed for warehousing and saving*. What's interesting is that it's the same word used in Exodus 2:3 to describe the little "ark" of bulrushes that Moses' mother placed him in and then set afloat on the Nile River.

Keep in mind that Moses was the one documenting the story of Noah in Genesis, and as he did, he surely reflected on his own story and the time his life was saved in the little ark made by his mom and dad. By faith, they made an ark to the saving of Moses' life. They trusted God that the currents of the Nile would carry Moses to a place of safety and deliverance. With this personal knowledge, Moses selected the word *kibotos* — translated here as "ark" — and used it in the Genesis account.

Hebrews 11:7 says Noah urgently built the Ark "to the saving of his house." A better translation of this phrase in Greek would be *for the explicit purpose of saving his own household*.

God Gave Noah the 'Inside Scoop' and He Fully Obeyed

Returning to Genesis 6:13-15, the Bible says, "And God said unto Noah, The end of all flesh is come before me; for the earth is filled with violence through them; and, behold, I will destroy them with the earth. Make thee an ark of gopher wood; rooms shalt thou make in the ark, and shalt pitch it within and without with pitch. And this is the fashion which thou shalt make it of: The length of the ark shall be three hundred cubits, the breadth of it fifty cubits, and the height of it thirty cubits."

As we've noted in previous lessons, Noah walked with God habitually and found favor in His eyes (see Genesis 6:9). Consequently, God confided in Noah and prophetically warned him of what was coming. Noah listened as God began to lay out step-by-step instructions on what he and his family needed to do to save themselves from the ensuing Great Deluge.

How did Noah respond? The answer is clear:

Thus did Noah; according to all that God commanded him, so did he.
— **Genesis 6:22**

Noah and his family were careful to obey everything God had instructed them to do, and when they had finished the Ark, the Bible says:

And the Lord said unto Noah, Come thou and all thy house into the ark; for thee have I seen righteous before me in this generation.
— **Genesis 7:1**

There was something different about Noah from everyone else in his generation. He had a reverential fear and awe of God and obeyed what the Lord told him. This is a fact that is woven all through Genesis 6, 7, 8, and 9. For example, in Genesis 7:5, it says:

And Noah did according unto all that the Lord commanded him.

Friend, God is looking for modern-day Noahs. He is searching the earth to identify people who are walking in sync with His Spirit, obeying His instructions. Scripture says, "…The eyes of the Lord run to and fro throughout the whole earth, to show Himself strong on behalf of those whose heart is loyal to Him…" (2 Chronicles 16:9 *NKJV*).

Do you have ears to hear what God is saying? If so, are you fully obeying what the Holy Spirit has instructed you to do? In these last days, walking in obedience is essential for you to thrive in hard times. You must determine that you will fully obey whatever the Lord tells you to do. And "If ye be willing and obedient, ye shall eat the good of the land" (Isaiah 1:19).

Just as Noah was obedient, you need to be obedient to the Lord to sail through these times!

Questions and Answers With Rick Renner

In the program, Rick answered the following question from one of our viewers.

Q. What was the real shape of the cross?

A. In answer to this question, Rick said, "We read about the cross in John 19:17 where the Bible says: 'And he [Jesus] bearing his cross went forth into a place called the place of a skull, which is called in the Hebrew Golgotha.'"

Here, the word "cross" is the Greek word *stauros*, which describes *an upright, pointed stake that was used for the punishment of criminals.* This word was used to denote those who were hung up, impaled, or beheaded and then publicly displayed and was always used in connection with public execution.

Of course, most of us think of a cross that is shaped like a plus sign, but in the ancient Roman world, that's not what a cross looked like. The plus sign-shaped cross is a later version created by painters in the Middle Ages.

The cross during Christ's time was actually T-shaped, and the victim carried the top part — or beam — on his shoulders as he walked to the place of crucifixion. He was then nailed to the crossbeam, which was then hoisted upward with the body of the victim and dropped onto the upright post. Thus, the real shape of Jesus' cross was not like a plus sign but T-shaped.

In our next lesson, we will look at a very important factor in our obedience to Christ, and that is refusing to bow to the opinion of others.

STUDY QUESTIONS

> **Study to shew thyself approved unto God, a workman that needeth not to be ashamed, rightly dividing the word of truth.**
> **— 2 Timothy 2:15**

1. God knows the future and what is coming in the days ahead, and He knows what actions you need to take to be prepared. The key to receiving the inside, "prophetic scoop" like Noah is to get close to God and listen for His voice daily. What do these verses tell you about hearing from the Lord regarding what is coming in the days ahead?
   - Psalm 25:12-14
   - Amos 3:7
   - Hebrews 11:6
   - John 15:15 and 16:13-15
   - 1 Corinthians 2:9,10
2. *Obedience* is faith in action! It is doing the deeds God is directing us to do. Without obedient actions, our faith is dead. What do your actions show about your level of obedience to God? Carefully read through James 2:14-26 and write down what the Holy Spirit reveals to you.
3. According to Matthew 5:16, John 5:36, and First Peter 2:12 and 15, how do our obedient actions impact the lives of those around us? Can you think of someone's godly actions that really touched your life? If so, what did they do?

PRACTICAL APPLICATION

> But be ye doers of the word, and not hearers only, deceiving your own selves.
> —James 1:22

1. Hebrews 11:7 reveals that the motivating factor in Noah's life was the *fear of the Lord*. What do you understand "the fear of the Lord" to be?
2. Whether this is new to you or you've heard lots of teaching on it already, take some time to dive into these verses on the importance and blessings that come with the fear of the Lord.
   - **The Fear of the Lord Explained:**
     Deuteronomy 10:12,13; Psalm 34:11-14; Proverbs 8:13; 10:27; 14:26,27
   - **The Essence of the Fear of the Lord:**
     Psalm 111:10 and Proverbs 1:7; 9:10; 15:33

- **The Blessings of the Fear of the Lord:**
  Psalm 25:12; 31:19; 34:7,9,10; 103:13-18; 147:11 and
  Proverbs 14:26; 19:23; 22:4; 29:25

LESSON 8

TOPIC

Do Other People's Opinions Bother You?

SCRIPTURES

1. **Matthew 24:37** — But as the days of Noe [Noah] were, so shall also the coming of the Son of man be.
2. **Genesis 7:16,17** — And they that went in, went in male and female of all flesh, as God had commanded him: and the Lord shut him in. And the flood was forty days upon the earth; and the waters increased, and bare up the ark, and it was lift up above the earth.
3. **Hebrews 11:6** — But without faith it is impossible to please him….
4. **Hebrews 10:32,33** — But call to remembrance the former days, in which, after ye were illuminated, ye endured a great fight of afflictions; partly, whilst ye were made a gazingstock both by reproaches and afflictions….

GREEK WORDS

1. "without" — χωρίς (*choris*): without, as being outside of a specific place
2. "illuminated" — φωτίζω (*photidzo*): to illuminate; the impression of a brilliant flash of light that leaves a permanent and lasting impression
3. "endured" — ὑπομένω (*hupomeno*): to stay or to abide; to remain in one's spot; to keep a position; to resolve to maintain territory gained; in a military sense, it pictures soldiers ordered to maintain their positions even in the face of opposition; to defiantly stick it out regardless of pressures mounted against it; staying power; hang-in-there power; the attitude that holds out, holds on, outlasts, perseveres, and hangs in

there, never giving up, refusing to surrender to obstacles, and turning down every opportunity to quit; it pictures one who is under a heavy load but refuses to bend, break, or surrender because he is convinced that the territory, promise, or principle under assault rightfully belongs to him

4. "affliction" — **πάθημα** (*pathema*): a strong emotional struggle; emotional or mental agony
5. "gazingstock" — **θεατρίζω** (*theatridzo*): theater; to observe, to watch, to study, to scrutinize, or to bring upon the stage for all to see; pictures spectators in the theater watching a scenario being played before them; on the edge of their seats, spectators wait for the actors to make a mistake or forget a line so they can scorn, ridicule him, and make fun of him; it can be interpreted to bring on to the stage in order to scorn, to scoff at, to shame, sneer at, and to publicly humiliate; spectacle

SYNOPSIS

The calling on Noah — and his family — was a task like no other. It's not every day, or even every century, that someone is tapped by the Almighty to build a warehouse that will float on water to save his family and preserve a sample of all the animals of the earth and air. Yet, Noah was unique, and he not only listened to God but also obeyed God, doing all he had been instructed to do.

On hearing this remarkable story, one would certainly ask, "What were the neighbors — both near and far — saying about Noah?" Think about it: Noah and his family had a 500-plus-foot boat project parked in their yard for 100 years. Up until then, no one had seen rain, nor were they aware of the concept of raging floodwaters.

It's safe to say that Noah and his family became the laughingstock of the community, likely being mocked and ridiculed daily. (The Noah jokes that people came up with must have been some of the funniest one-liners anyone had ever heard!) But regardless of the negative opinions of others, Noah and his family remained faithful to their calling. Likewise, we, too, must stay faithful to the task God has called us to, even in the face of sneers, jeers, and threats. If we'll stick with what we know is right and obey the Lord, He will enable us to float on the sea of destruction in these last days.

The emphasis of this lesson:

Noah was a preacher of righteousness, but the people who heard him were resistant to his message and would not turn from their wicked ways. He and his family were probably mocked, laughed at, and made a gazingstock. But that didn't stop them from staying in their place of faith and fulfilling their God-given assignment.

The Rediscovery of Noah's Ark Is a Sobering Symbol Pointing to the End of Days

The ruins of Noah's Ark are still visible today in the mountains of Ararat, embedded in the earth of a lower slope called Mount Judi in eastern Turkey. With all the recent resurgence of interest in the Ark, it is a sobering reminder of what Jesus declared in Matthew 24:37: "But as the days of Noe [Noah] were, so shall also the coming of the Son of man be."

What was going on in the world just before the Flood will be going on again just before the coming of Christ. Those are Jesus' words — not man's opinion. Rick meticulously unpacks these happenings in his cutting-edge series entitled *Fallen Angels, Giants, Monsters, and the World Before the Flood*, which you can find at **renner.org**.

No doubt, we are living in crazy times. In fact, everything the Holy Spirit prophesied through Paul in Second Timothy 3 is happening right before our eyes! You can learn all about these end-time signs in Rick's 15-part series called *Last-Days Survival Guide*, which is also available at **renner.org**.

In any case, the Bible tells us that after a century of building, the Ark was completed, "And they that went in, went in male and female of all flesh, as God had commanded him: and the Lord shut him in. And the flood was forty days upon the earth; and the waters increased, and bare up the ark, and it was lift up above the earth" (Genesis 7:16,17).

This means Noah, his family, and all the animals literally floated on the waters of destruction, which is exactly what God will enable us to do as we obey His instructions in these last-of-the-last days.

Despite the People's Response, Noah and His Family Stayed Committed to God's Call

In Second Peter 2:5 (*GNT*), it says, "God did not spare the ancient world, but brought the flood on the world of godless people; the only ones he saved were Noah, who preached righteousness, and seven other people." It seems that while Noah was building the big boat, he was also warning people to repent, get right with God, and get on the Ark so their lives would be spared from the coming global flood that would destroy all life.

Can you just imagine the negative opinions and the pushback Noah must have received from his message? He may have even been questioned on occasion by his wife, his sons, and his sons' wives. "Are you absolutely *sure* you heard from God?" they probably asked as they continued to shake off the daily insults and verbal attacks from the godless culture around them. Through it all, Noah and his family stayed the course and finished the Ark.

This brings us to another pivotal moment in their journey — the moment the animals began to show up. Can't you just see it? Busting through the brush from the north, south, east, and west, a steady procession of wildlife of all kinds making their way up to and then into the Ark. Strangely, they came as couples — male and female of every form of fowl, beast of burden, and creepy crawly thing. Again, how did Noah's neighbors respond to the sudden appearance of all these animals? Did they roar in laughter? Or were they left speechless as lions and llamas, bears and bison, alligators and antelopes came out of nowhere, as if on cue to claim their place in Noah's zoo?

Regardless of how the people responded, Noah and his family remained on task, continuing to guide the animals into their place of safety in the Ark. How did Noah get the animals? God brought them to him! Genesis 6:20 (*NKJV*) says, "Of the birds after their kind, of animals after their kind, and of every creeping thing of the earth after its kind, two of every kind **will come to you** to keep them alive." Indeed, the whole thing was a supernatural work of God!

What It Means To Be 'Without Faith'

Interestingly, just before the writer of Hebrews talks about the faith of Noah, he makes a powerful declaration about faith itself. He said:

> **But without faith it is impossible to please him [God]....**
> **— Hebrews 11:6**

For many Christians, this is a familiar verse, but it is often misunderstood. Rather than talking about having — or possessing — faith, this passage is talking about *how* and *where* faith operates. The key is understanding the meaning of the word "without." It is the Greek word *choris*, which means *without*, as being *outside of a specific place*. Thus, a more literal translation of this part of Hebrews 11:6 would be, "But *on the outside of faith*, it is impossible to please Him...."

Essentially, faith is an assignment from God, and as long as you stay *within* your assignment, you're going to please Him. The fact is, there are always pressures trying to pull you out of a place of faith — including the negative voices of people's opinions seeking to intimidate and scare you out of what God has asked you to do.

Consider Noah. His place of faith was to build an Ark to the specifications God gave him, and he needed to stay in his God-given assignment for a *very long time* — about 100 years to be exact. More than likely, there were times when Noah's wife asked, "Noah, are you absolutely *sure* God has spoken to you and asked you to do this?" Possibly even his sons said, "Uh, Dad...We're giving our lives for all this. Do you know *without question* that God spoke to you?" The truth is, there were forces all around Noah that were pulling on him and trying to move him out of his place of faith.

This was especially true of the people in the region around him. They had never heard of or seen a flood, an ark being built, or the parade of animals that gathered in Noah's community. These things seemed extremely bizarre to all the bystanders. Did people laugh at Noah and his sons? Did they ridicule him and his family and make nasty, derogatory jokes? It's almost a certainty. Nevertheless, he prophesied that a worldwide flood was going to come and destroy the earth and everything in it.

Regardless of the world's criticism, the questions from his family, and even the personal concerns that may have weighed on his own mind, Noah rejected it all and chose to stay in his place of faith. As a result, he saved his family, and his obedience is why we are here today.

When God Gives You an Assignment, You Are 'Illuminated'

Staying in your place of faith takes total commitment and every ounce of spiritual strength the Holy Spirit provides. Noah knew he had to put aside all the negative opinions of others about what he was doing. Likewise, he had to turn a deaf ear to all the jokes people were making and get into alignment with God's plan for his life. This brings us to an important verse of Scripture in Hebrews 10:32, which says:

> **But call to remembrance the former days, in which, after ye were illuminated, ye endured a great fight of afflictions.**

Notice the word "illuminated," which is the Greek word *photidzo*. It means *to illuminate*, and it carries the impression of *a brilliant flash of light that leaves a permanent and lasting impression*. Here, the writer is letting us know that when the Holy Spirit opens our eyes to the bright light of God's truth, we experience a great fight of affliction.

When God spoke to Noah and told him of the coming destruction and gave him the way of escape through the Ark, Noah was "illuminated!" God's words were like a brilliant flash of light that left an impression on him. In that moment, he was permanently changed. Noah knew what God had called him to do, so he went and told his wife, his sons, and his daughters-in-law, and eventually the people in his community saw it in his actions.

But with that illumination from the Lord, there also came a great fight of affliction. According to Hebrews 10:32, that is what will happen when God illuminates us with truth. The truth is, not everyone is going to rejoice when you receive a heavenly assignment, so it's wise to be prepared to endure the opposition that will very likely come your way.

Once We're Illuminated, We Need 'Endurance'

Again, the Bible says, "…After ye were illuminated, ye endured a great fight of afflictions" (Hebrews 10:32). The word "endured" here is a form of the Greek word *hupomeno*, which means *to stay or abide*. It can be translated *to remain in one's spot*; *to keep a position*, or *to resolve to maintain territory gained*. In a military sense, it pictures soldiers ordered to maintain their positions, even in the face of opposition. It means *to defiantly stick it out regardless of pressures mounted against it.*

Moreover, this word *hupomeno* — translated here as "endured" — can also be described as *staying power* or *hang-in-there power*. It is *the attitude that holds out, holds on, outlasts, perseveres, and hangs in there, never giving up, refusing to surrender to obstacles, and turning down every opportunity to quit.* It pictures one who is under a heavy load but refuses to bend, break, or surrender because he is convinced that the territory, promise, or principle under assault rightfully belongs to him.

So when the Bible talks about enduring a great fight of affliction, it means we have to make a decision to hold on, persevere, and stay in our place of faith, never surrendering to the enemy or quitting, regardless of the pressures or the afflictions that come against us.

In Hebrews 10:32, the word "affliction" is the Greek word *pathema*, which is where we get the words "pathos" and "pathology." It describes *suffering* and specifically deals with *a strong emotional struggle* or *emotional or mental agony*. The use of this word here indicates that one of the greatest fights we face when the Holy Spirit illuminates truth to us is the mental and emotional struggle of people not agreeing with what we believe God has told us to do. This can be especially agonizing when those who disagree with us are our family members and close friends.

Many times, it is easier to deal with personal doubts or even with the devil's assaults than it is to deal with your family and close friends when they disagree with you. Their negative opinion of or withdrawal from you results in a great fight of "affliction," which again is a kind of *pathos* or *mental agony* or an *emotional struggle* that can be very difficult to overcome.

People Are Watching… So Give Them a Show They'll Never Forget!

One of the primary forms of affliction that we face is public scrutiny. This unsolicited examination is actually mentioned in Hebrews 10:33, which says, "Partly, whilst ye were made a gazingstock both by reproaches and afflictions…."

In this verse, the word "gazingstock" is the Greek word *theatridzo*, which is the term for *a theater*, and it means *to observe, to watch, to study, to scrutinize*, or *to bring upon the stage for all to see*. It pictures spectators in the theater watching a scenario being played before them as they sit on the edge of their seats. In this case, these spectators are waiting for the actors to make a mistake or forget a line so they can scorn, ridicule, and make fun of them. This word *theatridzo* can also be interpreted *to bring on to the stage in order to scorn, to scoff at, to shame, to sneer at, and to publicly humiliate*. Very often, this word is translated as simply *spectacle*.

What the writer of Hebrews is telling us is that the moment you receive a word from God giving you direction or illumination of truth and you announce it, it's as if people begin to buy seats to the show. They want to watch and see if you're really going to do what you say God has told you to do.

Take Noah, for example. God revealed to him that there was going to be a global flood, and he announced it. People then began talking about it. "What is rain?" they asked. "Is there really going to be a flood? Noah said he's going to build an ark. What's an ark? And what's this old man talking about?"

As soon as the words of illumination left Noah's mouth, people began to buy seats to the theater of Noah's life and watch to see if what he said was really going to happen. Would he follow through? Or would he give up along the way? In the same way, when you make a declaration of faith and speak what God is showing you, your life becomes like a theater for people to watch.

When that happens, you can't change it. The only thing you can do about it is make a decision that if people are going to buy a seat to watch your life, give them the best performance they've ever seen! With God's grace, do your very best to obey His instructions and demonstrate how faith works. Be faithful to follow through on His calling — all the way to the end.

Every time you carry a God-given assignment through to fulfillment, it shows others that it can be done. Your success story becomes an encouragement for someone else who just received an illumination from God.

Friend, if something or someone is trying to pull you out of your place of faith, pray and ask God for His strength to help you push past all the trials, troubles, and negative opinions of others. Receive God's strength to pull yourself up and stay in alignment with the assignment He's given you. Make a decision to shut your eyes and ears to all distractions and stay focused on the task He's put in front of you.

Noah and his family had to resist a lot of negative voices and take a stand against the opinion of the world. But the result was more than worth it when Noah and his family safely floated on the waters of destruction and all the negative voices were silenced.

Questions and Answers With Rick Renner

In the program, Rick answered the following question from one of our viewers.

Q. What is 'weeping and gnashing of teeth'?

A. Multiple times throughout the gospels, Jesus makes a statement describing what is going to happen to those who are disobedient, wicked, and unfaithful. He said, "…[They] shall be cast out into outer darkness; there shall be weeping and gnashing of teeth" (Matthew 8:12). We also find this expression in Matthew 22:13; 24:51; 25:30; and Luke 13:28.

This is a phrase most people in Jesus' day would have understood. In the ancient world, if the leaders of a city suspected someone was guilty of wrongdoing, but they weren't positively sure, they would bind him with ropes and put him just outside the city walls in what was referred to as "outer darkness."

Now, this was a place of great weeping and sheer torment because on most nights, lions would roam that area, roaring and looking for food. Those who were bound and sitting in the outer darkness were so afraid of being consumed by the lions that they would usually gnash and grind their teeth down to nothing throughout the night. The next morning when the leaders returned, if they found the person still alive, they believed it meant he was not guilty.

In our next lesson, we will examine how to act fearlessly when God speaks a word of direction.

STUDY QUESTIONS

Study to shew thyself approved unto God, a workman that needeth not to be ashamed, rightly dividing the word of truth.
— 2 Timothy 2:15

1. Ridicule, name-calling, and the negative opinions of others are all forms of persecution that Noah and his family likely endured. Although we may not like to talk about it, being treated harshly by others is a part of being a Christian. Carefully comb through these passages and see if you can identify the *good* that God will bring out of the bad things you endure.
   - Hebrews 5:8
   - 1 Peter 4:1
   - 2 Timothy 3:11,12
   - 2 Corinthians 12:9,10
   - Romans 8:35-39
2. The Bible says that when the Lord illuminates our life with truth, we are confronted with affliction that requires endurance (*see* Hebrews 10:32). Take a moment to carefully reread the section on our need for "endurance" — the Greek word *hupomeno*. What truth is the Holy Spirit *illuminating* to you from the meaning of this word?
3. Essentially, to "stay in faith" is to *stay in an assignment God has given you*. As long as you stay *within* your assignment, you're going to please God. Do you know what is your present assignment from God (it may be more than one)? Are you *within* (inside of) or *without* (outside of) your place of faith?

PRACTICAL APPLICATION

> **But be ye doers of the word, and not hearers only, deceiving your own selves.**
> **—James 1:22**

1. It's very likely that Noah and his family were ridiculed and rejected by many in society for their righteous stand and for claiming they had heard from God. What kind of negative opinions and pushback have you received from others because of your decision to follow Jesus and live according to His Word?
2. What outside pressures do you find most difficult to deal with? Is it harder to handle pushback from your family and friends, strangers online, or the people you run into in your daily life? What hope did this lesson offer you to help you next time you're facing that opposition?

3. Can you remember a "*photidzo* moment" in your life — a time when the Holy Spirit "illuminated" truth or gave you clear direction? What did He show you? How did you respond? How has it left a lasting impression on you and affected those around you?
4. If you're a follower of Christ, you have likely been made the "gazingstock" of others at some point or another. But have you ever made *others* a gazingstock? Have you been a spectator of someone, watching and waiting for them to make a mistake so you could gloat and make fun of them? If so, who was it? Why do you think you did it? If you need to, take a few minutes to repent, ask God to forgive you, and pray for the person you looked down on. That fresh start will make a huge difference in your soul going forward!

LESSON 9

TOPIC

Acting With Fearlessness When God Speaks!

SCRIPTURES

1. **Genesis 7:16,17** — And they that went in, went in male and female of all flesh, as God had commanded him: and the Lord shut him in. And the flood was forty days upon the earth; and the waters increased, and bare up the ark, and it was lift up above the earth.
2. **2 Timothy 1:7** — For God hath not given us the spirit of fear; but of power, and of love, and of a sound mind.

GREEK WORDS

1. "not" — emphatically not
2. "given" — δίδωμι (*didomi*): to give, to hand over, to pass to another, to transmit, or to transfer
3. "spirit of fear" — πνεῦμα δειλίας (*pneuma deilias*): the word πνεῦμα (*pneuma*) means spirit, and can depict an attitude; the word δειλία (*deilia*) depicts cowardice or timidity; as a phrase, an attitude or spirit of cowardice and timidity

4. "but" — ἀλλά (*alla*): but; on the contrary or all the way to the opposite end of the spectrum
5. "power" — δύναμις (*dunamis*): explosive, superhuman power that comes with enormous energy and produces phenomenal, extraordinary, and unparalleled results; depicts "mighty deeds" that are impressive, incomparable, and beyond human ability to perform; used to denote the felt effects of an earthquake, hurricane, or tornado; depicts the full might of advancing Roman armies
6. "love" — ἀγάπη (*agape*): a divine love that gives and gives even if it's never responded to, thanked, or acknowledged; a love so profound that it knows no limits or boundaries in how far, wide, high, and deep it will go to show that love to its recipient
7. "sound mind" — σωφρονισμός (*sophronismos*): a compound of σῴζω (*sodzo*) and φρήν (*phren*); the word σῴζω (*sodzo*) denotes deliverance, healing, prosperity, safety, soundness, and well-being; the word φρήν (*phren*) pictures the mind or intellect; as a compound, it means to be of sound mind; to be reasonable; to be balanced and levelheaded in the way one thinks; to think clearly; to think rationally; a mind that has been delivered, rescued, revived, salvaged, and protected and which now is safe and secure

SYNOPSIS

In the valley flood plain, just below the landing place of Noah's Ark in eastern Turkey, there is a very ancient building, which many scholars and researchers believe to be the place where Noah lived after disembarking the Ark. This would be where he became a "husbandman," or farmer, and planted a vineyard (*see* Genesis 9:20).

This ancient building dates to about 500 AD and appears to be an ancient Armenian and Byzantine church that was built on top of the ruins of Noah's home. The church was erected to commemorate the site where Noah and his family lived after the Flood.

Not far from this site is an ancient altar, which is marked off with stones that form a fence to keep people and animals from entering the area. Some believe this was the sacred place where Noah and his family made additional sacrifices to God as they worshiped Him from their heart.

If you think about it, the world was a scary place for Noah and his family — both before and after the Flood. Can you imagine what it was like to have the responsibility of replenishing the earth? This would include birthing and raising multiple sons and daughters as well as helping the animals get reacclimated to the new world. Noah and his family needed the wisdom and strength of God to fulfill their assignment — and so do we. If we will seek Him, He will deliver us from all fear (*see* Psalm 34:4) and give us the confidence we need to sail through these turbulent times by the power of His Spirit!

The emphasis of this lesson:

Fear is a spirit sent out by Satan to paralyze and incapacitate you from fulfilling your divine assignments. But God has not given you a spirit of fear — He's given you His very own Holy Spirit of power, love, and a sound mind. By embracing His Spirit and resisting fear, you can boldly move forward and accomplish all God has called you to do!

The Pre-Flood World Was Dreadful Beyond Imagination

The days in which Noah lived were exceedingly wicked. The Bible says before the Flood, the earth was filled with violence and all flesh had become corrupt (*see* Genesis 6:5,11-13). The reason for the intense evil and perversity is found in Genesis 6:4 (*NIV*), which says, "The Nephilim were on the earth in those days — and also afterward — when the sons of God went to the daughters of humans and had children by them. They were the heroes of old, men of renown."

The word *Nephilim* is from the Hebrew word which means *the fallen ones*, and it describes the *giants* who were born out of the sexual union between the fallen angels and certain women of earth. These strange activities are confirmed in the Septuagint, which is the Greek translation of the Old Testament, and is also documented by ancient rabbinical writings, Early Church history, as well as the *Book of Enoch*.

These giants were hybrid beings — part angelic being and part human. We know from early history that when the natural food supply no longer satisfied them, they resorted to cannibalism. Not only did giants eat other giants, but they also began eating the flesh and drinking the blood of humans. Thus, the level of violence and barbarism during those days was horrific.

Josephus, the renowned Jewish historian, verifies the illicit relations between the sons of God (fallen angels) and daughters of men and added this interesting fact:

> But Noah was very uneasy at what they did; and, being displeased at their conduct, persuaded them to change their dispositions and their acts for the better; but, seeing that they did not yield to him, but were slaves to their wicked pleasures, he was afraid they would kill him, together with his wife and children, and those they had married; so he departed out of that land.[1]

Clearly, there was much for Noah and his family to be afraid of, but somewhere around this time, God spoke to Noah and revealed to him the coming destruction of the world. The Lord also gave him detailed instructions regarding the building of the Ark and the rescue mission for the birds of the air and the beasts of the field. As we've noted, the task of building the Ark and gathering the animals could have been very overwhelming for Noah and his family. But with God's help, they were able to conquer fear and accomplish their assignment.

Fear Is a Spirit That Is Not From God

Jesus said that the condition of the world just before His coming would be the same as it was in the days of Noah (*see* Matthew 24:37). Indeed, the times in which we're living can be quite frightening, but the Bible says, "God hath not given us the spirit of fear; but of power, and of love, and of a sound mind" (2 Timothy 1:7). This amazing promise is jam-packed with meaning.

First, it says, "God hath *not*," and the word "not" is important. In Greek, it means *emphatically not*. It is the equivalent of saying, "God has *emphatically not* given us a spirit of fear...." The word "given" is a form of the Greek word *didomi*, which means *to give, to hand over, to pass to another, to transmit*, or *to transfer*. The use of this word tells us that God has categorically not transferred or passed on to us a spirit of fear.

This brings us to the phrase "spirit of fear," which is a translation of the words *pneuma deilias*. The word *pneuma* is the term for *spirit* and can also depict *an attitude*. The word *deilia* depicts *cowardice* or *timidity*. As a phrase, "spirit of fear" describes *an attitude or spirit of cowardice and timidity*. When you have an attitude or spirit of cowardice and timidity, it paralyzes and incapacitates you. Instead of moving forward and doing what God has called you to do, fear will immobilize you and can even cause you to retreat into a posture of self-preservation.

Keep in mind *fear is really a spirit*. That is what the apostle Paul calls it. Have you ever watched a movie and felt fear when something terrible was suddenly depicted on the screen? Or have you been in a challenging situation, and suddenly fearful thoughts began to fill your mind, making you feel afraid and void of strength for the task? That is a spirit of fear. Fear will distort your thinking and make you believe things that will never happen in a million years. If you yield — or give in to — a spirit of fear, you will never be able to fulfill what God is calling you to do.

Again, fear is not from God but from the enemy. It is a spiritual problem that must be dealt with *spiritually*. When a spirit of fear comes against you, you are to submit yourself to God and resist fear (*see* James 4:7; 1 Peter 5:9). As you stand your ground against that demonic spirit and tell it to go in Jesus' name, it has to leave!

God Has Given You His Spirit of Power!

Looking once more at Second Timothy 1:7, it says, "For God hath not given us the spirit of fear; but of power, and of love, and of a sound mind." Notice the word "but" — the Greek word *alla*. Although it means *but*, it would better be translated *on the contrary* or *all the way to the opposite end of the spectrum*.

Rather than give us a spirit of fear, God has given us His Holy Spirit of "power." This word "power" is the Greek word *dunamis*, which describes *explosive, superhuman power that comes with enormous energy and produces phenomenal, extraordinary, and unparalleled results*. It depicts "mighty deeds" that are impressive, incomparable, and beyond human ability to perform. That is what God has given *you!*

Furthermore, this word *dunamis* — translated here as "power" — was also used to denote *the felt effects of an earthquake, hurricane,* or *tornado*. It is the same word used by the Greeks and Romans to depict *the full might of advancing Roman armies*. Again, that is the kind of Spirit God has given you — it is His very own Spirit Who is permanently living inside you (*see* 1 Corinthians 3:16; 6:19).

Friend, you have the power of God in you to blow things out of the way like a hurricane, shake things up like an earthquake, and march forward in might like an advancing army. Your job is to resist and reject fear and embrace and activate God's power through your words and actions of obedience.

You Are Also Equipped With God's Love and a Sound Mind

In addition to power, God has also given you His "love." In Greek, this is the marvelous word *agape*, which depicts *a divine love that gives and gives even if it's never responded to, thanked, or acknowledged*. It is *a love so profound that it knows no limits or boundaries in how far, wide, high, and deep it will go to show that love to its recipient*. First John 4:18 (*AMPC*) says:

> **There is no fear in love [dread does not exist], but full-grown (complete, perfect) love turns fear out of doors and expels every trace of terror!...**

Along with God's amazing love, Paul says He's also given you a "sound mind." This is the Greek word *sophronismos*, which is a compound of the words *sodzo* and *phren*. The word *sodzo* denotes *deliverance, healing, prosperity, safety, soundness, and well-being*; and the word *phren* pictures *the mind or intellect*. As a compound, the word *sophronismos* means *to be of sound mind*; *to be reasonable*; or *to be balanced and levelheaded in the way one thinks*. It can be translated *to think clearly* or *to think rationally*. It is the picture of *a mind that has been delivered, rescued, revived, salvaged, and protected and which now is safe and secure*.

Friend, that's the kind of mind God gave you — one that thinks clearly and rationally. A fearful mind is irrational and begins to imagine things happening to you that will never happen, but the possibility of them seems very real when you're being controlled by a spirit of fear. But God didn't give you a spirit of fear — He gave you His very own Holy Spirit of *power*, *love*, and *a sound mind*. Praise His mighty Name!

Push Fear Aside and Press Forward by Faith!

Noah and his family could have quickly and easily given place to a spirit of fear. They were living at the time when fallen angels were cohabiting with women on earth and birthing giants. These hybrid beings were extremely violent and barbaric and caused humanity and all living creatures to become corrupt. Without question, all this was a source of great fear.

At the same time, Noah was processing God's prophetic announcement that the world was going to be destroyed by a flood, and that he and his family were to build an ark. To accomplish this huge assignment required tremendous resources, manpower, and years of sacrificial work. God also instructed Noah to oversee the gathering of two of every kind of animal and bird, along with the food provisions that would be needed by everyone that would be on the Ark. Again, these tasks likely seemed impossible at times, and Noah and his family could have certainly become filled with anxiety, worry, and fear, but they didn't. Instead, they fearlessly tackled the assignment that God gave them to do.

A similar situation took place when the children of Israel were on the verge of entering the Promised Land. At that time, God spoke to Joshua and told him three times to *be strong and courageous* (*see* Joshua 1:6,7,9). He knew that Joshua would face extremely challenging situations and that the daily choice to be strong and courageous would be what he needed to effectively resist fear and embrace faith. Interestingly, when Joshua finally stood in front of the people of Israel and called them to action, they answered Joshua, "Whatever you have commanded us we will do, and wherever you send us we will go. ...Only be strong and courageous!'" (Joshua 1:16,18 *NIV*). Amazingly, the people repeated the same words to Joshua that God Himself had spoken.

Friend, for you to move forward fearlessly in these last days and do what God has called you to do, you, too, will have to be strong and courageous. The good news is that "God has not given us a spirit of fear, but of power and of love and of a sound mind" (2 Timothy 1:7 *NKJV*). So you have everything you need to do anything God has called you to do!

Just as Noah and his family got into the Ark and were lifted up above the earth as the flood waters increased (*see* Genesis 7:17), you, too, can dwell in the Ark of Safety — *Jesus* — and float on the sea of destruction in these last-of-the-last days. Through the power of the Holy Spirit, you can push fear aside and press forward into the future, fearlessly doing what God has called you to do!

Questions and Answers With Rick Renner

In the program, Rick answered the following question from one of our viewers.

Q. What did Jesus mean when He said 'You will tread on serpents and scorpions'?

A. In Luke 10:19, Jesus declared, "Behold, I give unto you power to tread on serpents and scorpions, and over all the power of the enemy: and nothing shall by any means hurt you." To begin to grasp what Jesus is saying, you need to understand that in the ancient world, serpents and scorpions were a real problem because they lay in the ruts of the roads, and most of the time travelers didn't know they were there until they were attacked by one.

Knowing that a serpent or scorpion could rise and strike you at any given moment while traveling created the perfect storm for fear to grip the minds and hearts of everyone on the road. Knowing this to be the case, Jesus called for His disciples before sending them out, and He said to them, "Behold, I give unto you power to tread on serpents and scorpions, and over all the power of the enemy: and nothing shall by any means hurt you" (Luke 10:19). Basically, He told His friends, "It doesn't matter what's hidden and waiting for you in the ruts of the roads because I'm giving you supernatural authority — even over serpents and scorpions and over all the power of the enemy!"

The word "over" is the Greek word *epi*, which means *upon* or *over*. It is a word that demonstrates the superior position Christ has given us over all the works of the enemy! So don't let fear numb you, paralyze you, incapacitate you, or turn you into a coward. Jesus has given you His power and authority to tread on the enemy, and not one single thing he brings against you will succeed!

In our final lesson, we will learn what it takes to receive the promises God made to us.

STUDY QUESTIONS

> Study to shew thyself approved unto God, a workman that
> needeth not to be ashamed, rightly dividing the word of truth.
> — 2 Timothy 2:15

1. Did you know that giants were eating human flesh and drinking blood? How do you think this affected the heart of God who made man in His image? (*Consider* Genesis 6:6.) What was the very first commandment God gave Noah and his family as they were exiting the Ark (*see* Genesis 9:4-6)? Can you see the connection between this stern command and the barbaric behavior that was happening in the pre-Flood world?
2. When you think about the kinds of fear Noah and his family were facing in the turbulent pre-Flood world and then in the post-Flood world, what do you think kept them from losing their minds? (*Consider* Psalm 28; 34:4; Second Timothy 1:7; Hebrews 13:5,6; and First John 4:18.)
3. Carefully reread the meaning of the word *agape*, the Greek word for "love," along with Romans 5:5-11. What part of God's *agape* love is He highlighting to you in this passage?

PRACTICAL APPLICATION

> But be ye doers of the word, and not hearers only,
> deceiving your own selves.
> —James 1:22

1. What often makes you feel fearful in everyday life? First John 4:18 (*AMPC*) says, "There is no fear in love [dread does not exist], but full-grown (complete, perfect) love turns fear out of doors and expels every trace of terror...." Take a moment to pray and ask the Holy Spirit to give you a fuller, deeper revelation of His perfect love for you and that His love will drive fear from your life.
2. Concerning "serpents and scorpions," what challenges and hidden dangers do you think are a modern-day equivalent in your own life? How are you encouraged, knowing that Jesus has given you authority to trample every attack from the enemy?
3. What do you remember most about Jesus' death and resurrection? Take a few minutes to remember what He went through on the Cross for you, letting the weight of His love wash over you.

---

[1] William Whiston, *The Works of Josephus*, trans. William Whiston (Hendrickson Publishers, Inc.: Peabody, MA, 1987,1994), 32.

LESSON 10

TOPIC
How To Receive the Promise God Made to You!

SCRIPTURES

1. **Genesis 7:16,17** — And they that went in, went in male and female of all flesh, as God had commanded him: and the Lord shut him in. And the flood was forty days upon the earth; and the waters increased, and bare up the ark, and it was lift up above the earth.
2. **Hebrews 6:12** — That ye be not slothful, but followers of them who through faith and patience inherit the promises.
3. **Hebrews 10:23** — Let us hold fast the profession of our faith without wavering; (for he is faithful that promised).
4. **Hebrews 10:35,36** — Cast not away therefore your confidence, which hath great recompence of reward. For ye have need of patience, that, after ye have done the will of God, ye might receive the promise.
5. **Hebrews 10:38,39** — Now the just shall live by faith: but if any man draw back, my soul shall have no pleasure in him. But we are not of them who draw back unto perdition; but of them that believe to the saving of the soul.

GREEK WORDS

1. "slothful" — **νωθρός** (*nothros*): dull, slow, and sluggish; something that has lost its speed or momentum; it conveys the idea of something that has lost the drive, thrust, impetus, pace, and speed it once possessed; the idea of one whose zeal has now dissipated; it denotes a person who has become disinterested and whose zeal has been replaced with a middle-of-the-road, take-it-or-leave-it mentality; it carries the idea of one who has a lethargic, lackadaisical, apathetic, indifferent, or lukewarm attitude; a non-achiever or a non-achieving attitude
2. "followers" — **μιμητής** (*mimetes*): one who imitates; a mimic; one who replicates what he sees someone else doing; used to describe actors who acted on the stage for their profession; implies the intentional

study of the deeds, words, actions, and thoughts of another person in order to replicate those attributes in one's own life; derivatives of this word are mimeograph, mime, pantomime, and mimic

3. "without wavering" — ἀκλινής (*aklines*): pictures something that does not bend; something that is fixed and unmoving; that which is stable and enduring; an attitude that is unbending, unchanging, fixed, stable, and unmoving

4. "confidence" — παρρησία (*parresia*): a bold, frank, forthright speech; extraordinary frankness

5. "recompense of reward" — μισθαποδοσία (*misthapodosia*): the word for money, salary, or a payment that is due; a full and complete recompense

6. "receive" — κομίζω (*komidzo*): to receive what is due; to receive what one has coming to him; payday

7. "draw back" — ὑποστέλλω (*hupostello*): to shrink back; one who is withdrawing, retreating, regressing, receding, backing away, backsliding, or recoiling from something; one who reverses his direction; to move backward instead of forward; to back off and retreat from an object, principle, or task

8. "perdition" — ἀπώλεια (*apoleia*): something rotten

SYNOPSIS

After warning Noah of the impending flood, God gave him a detailed plan of deliverance, and if he would obey the Lord's instructions, he and his family would be saved. This was God's promise to Noah, and because he had ears to hear what God was saying and he willingly obeyed, he and his family were saved from destruction just as God promised.

Likewise, when Noah and his wife, and his sons and their wives left the Ark, they heard God's command to "Be fruitful, and multiply, and replenish the earth" (Genesis 9:1). Again, they heard and obeyed God's voice and became the inheritors of the earth. If you think about it, all of us can trace our lineage back to Noah and his family. Their obedience thousands of years ago is still affecting our lives today.

In the same way, God has made promises to us, and if we will have ears to hear what He's saying and will obey, we, too, will inherit His promises, no matter how turbulent the season.

The emphasis of this lesson:

When we're assigned a long, difficult task like Noah's, it's so important to stay actively engaged and refuse to fall into slothfulness. As we seek to imitate and become more and more like Christ, faith and patience work together to bring about the fulfillment of God's promises.

The Ruins of Noah's Ark and His Post-Flood Home Are Still Here Today!

As we have noted throughout our study, there is a massive, ship-shaped formation embedded in the earth on the lower Ararat mountains in eastern Turkey. It is located on what is called Mount Judi, which is on the border of Iran and Armenia, and its dimensions fit those given to Noah by God in Genesis 6. After conducting numerous ERT scans, using ground-penetrating radar, and testing rock specimens, it has been determined that the mud-encased structure is indeed the manmade remnants of Noah's Ark.

In our last lesson, we saw that there is a very ancient structure in the valley just below the Ark's remains. It is the ruins of a centuries-old church, and it's located very near where the Ark came to rest. Many scholars, archeologists, and historians believe this was likely once the house where Noah lived and became a farmer after the Flood. One writer of ancient history noted that some early Armenian believers and even Byzantine Christians were so convinced that this was Noah's home that they converted the house into a church around 500 AD to memorialize the site.

Not far from this archaic homesite is an altar, which some believe is the very place where Noah and his family offered additional sacrifices to the Lord. There is an ancient stone wall that surrounds the altar, which seems to have been set up to keep animals and people from entering the area, as it is considered a sacred site.

Remember, once Noah and his family had finished constructing the Ark, the Bible says, "…They that went in, went in male and female of all flesh, as God had commanded him: and the Lord shut him in. And the flood was forty days upon the earth; and the waters increased, and bare up the ark, and it was lift up above the earth" (Genesis 7:16,17). Here we see that the same waters that annihilated everything on the earth elevated Noah, his family, and the animals in the Ark. Higher and higher they rose until they were literally floating on a sea of destruction.

Jesus said, "But as the days of Noah were, so shall also the coming of the Son of man be" (Matthew 24:37). The signs of Christ's soon return are everywhere, which means we are living in the timeframe that Jesus prophesied will be a mirror-image of Noah's day. As the waters of trouble rage and continue to rise around us, we can rise with them and float on the sea of destruction if we will abide in Jesus — our Ark of Safety — and hold tightly to God's Word.

Steps to Experiencing God's Promises

As we said in the introduction, Noah and his family were willing and obedient to the Lord's instructions, and as a result, they inherited the promises God made to them. Their life exemplifies several biblical steps we need to take in order to inherit the promises God has made to us.

Number 1: Don't Be Slothful

Hebrews 6:12 reveals a vital step to experiencing God's promises. It says, "That ye be not slothful, but followers of them who through faith and patience inherit the promises." In this verse, take note of the word "slothful." It is the Greek word *nothros*, and it describes something *dull, slow,* and *sluggish*. It is something that has *lost its speed or momentum* and conveys the idea of *one that has lost the drive, thrust, impetus, pace, and speed it once possessed.*

Moreover, it depicts *one whose zeal has now dissipated*, and it denotes *a person who has become disinterested and whose zeal has been replaced with a middle-of-the-road, take-it-or-leave-it mentality.* This word *nothros* — translated here as "slothful" — carries the idea of *one who has a lethargic, lackadaisical, apathetic, indifferent, or lukewarm attitude.* It describes *a non-achiever with a non-achieving attitude.*

Are you getting an image of a "slothful" person? It's someone who at one time had zeal and passion, but over time, they've developed "a take-it-or-leave-it" mentality. Very often, as a person waits for the promise of God to come to pass, they grow tired mentally, emotionally, and even spiritually. Gradually, often imperceptibly, they become lukewarm or slothful. The only way to overcome this dilemma is to work hard to keep your zeal stirred up.

More than likely, Noah — and each of his family members — had to deal with the temptation to become slothful. The Bible seems to indicate that he began building the Ark at age 500, and it says the Flood came when he was 600 (*see* Genesis 5:32; 6:10; 7:6). Hence, the construction took about 100 years, which is an extremely long time to stay focused and committed to any endeavor, much less one that no one understood. How do you think you would respond if you'd been given Noah's assignment? Do you think your zeal and drive would ever dwindle, especially in the face of exhaustion, ridicule, and spending all your resources to make it happen?

If God has spoken something to your heart and you can't seem to shake it, ask Him for the strength to maintain your zeal and remain in alignment with your assignment. You *can* resist the temptation to become slothful, and the key is found in Hebrews 6:12: "That ye be not slothful, but followers of them who through faith and patience inherit the promises."

Number 2: Be a Follower or Imitator of God

The word "followers" in Hebrews 6:12 is the remarkable Greek word *mimetes*, which describes *one who imitates*. It is where we get the word for *a mimic* and depicts *one who replicates what he sees someone else doing*. This word is used to describe *actors who acted on the stage for their profession*, and it implies *the intentional study of the deeds, words, actions, and thoughts of another person in order to replicate those attributes in one's own life*. The derivatives of this word are *mimeograph, mime, pantomime*, and *mimic*.

This word *mimetes* is the same word used in Ephesians 5:1, where the apostle Paul says, "Be ye therefore followers of God, as dear children." The word "followers" is the Greek word *mimetes*. Thus, this verse could be translated, *"Be an imitator of God, just as children mimic their father. Study His deeds, words, actions, and thoughts in order to replicate those attributes in your own life."*

So when Hebrews 6:12 says, "…Be not slothful, but followers of them who through faith and patience inherit the promises," it is instructing us to watch those who've gone before us and who've inherited the promises of God, and if we want the same results they received, to do what they did. In other words, carefully study their life and imitate their behavior. Do what they do and say what they say.

Now someone may say, "Well, that's just acting. Isn't that insincere?" Yes, it is acting, but it's not insincere if you truly want to live that way. For example, most children behave as their parents instruct them, but for a long time, their heart is not in it. Nevertheless, as they go through the motions of doing the right thing, it develops the discipline they need that creates a healthy desire. Eventually, the day comes when suddenly, that established discipline or habit of doing the right thing flips an internal switch and ignites their desire to do the right thing.

The idea of this word *mimetes*, which essentially means *to mimic and imitate someone*, is what it means to "...*Put on* the Lord Jesus Christ, and make no provision for the flesh, to fulfill its lusts" (Romans 13:14 *NKJV*).

Number 3: Let Faith and Patience Work Together

Looking once more at Hebrews 6:12, it says, "...Be not slothful, but followers of them who through faith and patience inherit the promises." Notice the latter part of the verse. It says that through *faith* and *patience* we inherit the promises of God. Please don't miss this as it is very important to see the connection between these two attributes.

You might say that faith and patience are the *parents* that give birth to the promises of God. You must have both of these active in your life to experience God's promises. What's interesting is that the word *faith* in Greek is usually very active, assertive, and moving forward. Hence, it would symbolize the role of the man.

In contrast, the word *patience* is usually more passive and enduring and takes on the feminine role. When the male component (faith) and the female component (patience) unite, the "baby" that is birthed is the promise of God, which becomes a reality. Said differently, faith acts as the initiator that actively moves forward and sows into the womb of patience, and when faith and patience become intertwined, they give birth to the promises of God.

Consider Noah. He believed what God said, and he began to actively move forward and do what God instructed. This is *faith* in action. But Noah also had to have *patience* (time, perseverance, and staying power to build the Ark, make it through the Flood, and rebuild the new world). Patience was needed for what he believed to be fully developed and come to pass in his life. The same holds true for you. When faith and patience are working together in your life, you will give birth to the promises of God.

Number 4: Hold Fast the Profession of Your Faith

Another important verse to help you understand how to experience the promises of God is Hebrews 10:23, which says, "Let us hold fast the profession of our faith without wavering; (for he is faithful that promised).

If you have a *King James Version*, the word "our" is likely italicized, which means it doesn't appear in the original Greek text. It simply says, "Let us hold fast the profession of faith…." This throws the door wide open so that whatever your profession of faith is, this verse applies to it. Therefore, we could translate it to say: "Let us hold fast the profession of faith [*whatever it is*] without wavering (for he is faithful that promised)."

The phrase "without wavering" is a transition of the Greek word *aklines*, which is from the word *klines*, the term for a *bed*. In this case, an *a* is attached to the front, which reverses or cancels the meaning. Hence, it literally means *without a bed*. When we insert this meaning into Hebrews 10:23, it is the equivalent of saying, "Let us hold fast to the profession of our faith *without going to bed on our faith*."

This word *alklines* depicts *something that does not bend* or *something that is fixed and unmoving*. It is the picture of *being stable and enduring*, and denotes *an attitude that is unbending, unchanging, fixed, stable, and unmoving*. Thus, the word *aklines* — translated here as "without wavering" — describes a person who never gives up or goes to bed on what he or she is believing God for. When you hold fast to your confession of faith, you stay actively engaged and don't allow yourself to become neutral, sluggish, or slothful; you retain your passion for what God told you to do.

Number 5: Cast Not Away Your Confidence

Hebrews 10:35 goes on to say, "Cast not away therefore your confidence, which hath great recompence of reward." The word "confidence" is a translation of the Greek word *parresia*, and it describes *a bold, frank, forthright kind of speech*. It depicts *one that is audacious or emboldened* and carries the idea of being *extraordinarily frank*. It means *daring to speak what one believes or thinks without hesitation — possibly even in the face of retribution*. Furthermore, it describes *boldness, assurance, and unashamed confidence*, and denotes *a frankness of speech that accompanies unflinching authority*.

And the reason we are to hold tightly to our confidence is because, "[it] hath great recompence of reward" (Hebrews 10:35). The phrase "recompense of reward" is from the Greek word *misthapodosia*, which is the term for *money, salary, or a payment that is due*. It is primarily used to denote *a payment, salary, or reward given for a job performed*. It can also describe *a full and complete recompense, settlement, or reparation*. It is a *reimbursement for an expense a person has paid out of his own pocket in order to get his job done*.

Here the writer of Hebrews is basically saying, "If you will hang on and continue to boldly confess your faith in God, payday is coming! He is going to reimburse you for everything you've given out."

Number 6: You Will Receive God's Promise

Then he added in the next verse, "For ye have need of patience, that, after ye have done the will of God, ye might receive the promise" (Hebrews 10:36). Notice the word "receive." In Greek, it is the word *komidzo*, which literally means *to receive what is due* or *to receive what one has coming to him*. The use of this word here is the equivalent of saying, "Whatever promise of God you've been declaring by faith — whatever you've been boldly speaking and believing God for — is coming to you. It is your *recompense* or *reward* that is on its way to you — as long as you refuse to be neutral, lackadaisical, or slothful."

Friend, if you continue to believe and speak the Word of God, allowing faith and patience to work together and refusing to go to bed on your faith, one day payday will arrive. The promise you have been waiting on and believing God for will become a reality in your life!

We Are Called To Live By Faith

When we come to Hebrews 10:38, we are given this vital instruction: "Now the just shall live by faith: but if any man draw back, my soul shall have no pleasure in him." In this verse, the phrase "draw back" is the Greek word *hupostello*, which means *to shrink back*. It pictures *one who is withdrawing, retreating, regressing, receding, backing away, backsliding, or recoiling from something*.

Furthermore, the word *hupostello* depicts *one who reverses his direction*. It carries the idea of *moving backward instead of forward*. Rather than staying actively engaged in faith, this person is *backing off and retreating from an object, principle, or task*. This shrinking back usually takes place gradually, one step at a time. As this person experiences one little discouragement after another, he releases his grip on his confession of faith.

The writer of Hebrews then immediately added, "But we are not of them who draw back unto perdition; but of them that believe to the saving of the soul" (Hebrews 10:39). Once again, we see the phrase "draw back" — the Greek word *huposteilo*. In this case, he is saying, "We are *not* the kind of people that *shrink back*, *withdraw*, or *retreat* from our position of faith." Specifically, he is saying, "But we are not of them who draw back unto *perdition*…" (Hebrews 10:39).

If Your Life Seems To 'Stink,' There's a Reason

Now the word "perdition" in Hebrews 10:39 is very important. It is the Greek word *apoleia*, and it pictures *something ruined, rotten, and decomposing*. It was used to describe *the stench of a decaying animal or a dead human body*. It denoted *a loathsome, putrid, vulgar, disgusting, and nauseating scent*, caused by *something in the process of perishing; something doomed, rotten, ruinous, or decaying*.

This word *apoleia* — translated here as "perdition" — gives us a vivid picture of what happens to a person who backs off or retreats from what God promised him. When he abandons his position of faith, his life begins to emit a terrible spiritual stench. His view of life — as well as his attitude toward those who are walking in faith — is marked by a nauseating cynicism and bitterness. If you've ever been there, you know how awful this condition can be.

To avoid living a rotten life that stinks, you need to maintain your confession of faith. This means praying to receive God's grace to act in patience, stay in faith, and confess His Word. His grace will also enable you to retain your passion and refuse to give up or back away from what He promised. Friend, payday is on the way!

Questions and Answers With Rick Renner

In the program, Rick answered the following question from one of our viewers.

Q. Are we supposed to deliberately eat and drink deadly things?

A. In Mark 16:17 and 18, Jesus gave several specific signs that we as believers can expect to see as we continue to trust in Him and His Word.

In verse 18, He said, "They shall take up serpents; and if they drink any deadly thing, it shall not hurt them…."

Keep in mind, Jesus spoke these words as He was dispatching the disciples — which includes us — to the ends of the world. He knew that as we take the Gospel to people in remote places, we would sometimes encounter dangerous things.

Therefore, when He made this promise in Mark 16:18, He wasn't actually telling us to physically pick up snakes or purposely drink poison. Instead, He was telling His disciples — both then and now — that if we run into a poisonous serpent or some other deadly situation, we are not to worry or be afraid, because He has given us divine protection against them. Likewise, if we happen to eat or drink anything toxic while we're obediently carrying out God's calling on our life, the Lord will protect us from it as well.

The key to experiencing Christ's supernatural protection — as well as floating on a sea of destruction in these last-of-the-last-days — is staying in faith. As you continue to patiently believe and speak the Word and refuse to give up, faith and patience will eventually give birth to the promises of God. If Noah could do it, you can do it too!

STUDY QUESTIONS

Study to shew thyself approved unto God, a workman that needeth not to be ashamed, rightly dividing the word of truth.
— 2 Timothy 2:15

1. How incredible was it to learn that there's a church built on Noah's old home site? What does Scripture say about the righteous person's legacy? (*See* Proverbs 10:7 and Psalm 112:6.)

2. It can be overwhelmingly exhausting to keep pursuing the goals God has placed in your heart — which is why so many fall into slothfulness. What does the Lord offer to do for us when we come to Him and ask for His help to keep on going? (*See* Isaiah 40:28-31 and Matthew 11:28-30.)

3. What does God promise He will do when we keep at it, day after day, week after week, year after year? (*See* Galatians 6:9,10; Hebrews 10:35-37; and Revelation 3:10-12.)

PRACTICAL APPLICATION

> But be ye doers of the word, and not hearers only,
> deceiving your own selves.
> —James 1:22

1. What parts of life (or your calling from God) tend to exhaust you the most? Take a minute to bring them to God in prayer — verbally or on paper — and ask Him to help you truly rest in His ability. Invite Him to give you His strength (grace) to keep going strong, despite the opposition (see James 4:6; Second Corinthians 9:8; and Psalm 84:11.)

2. Have you ever heard the term "fake it till you make it"? Sometimes when it comes to doing the right thing, we need to *act* like it LONG before we *feel* like it. Can you think of an instruction God gave you that you *just don't feel like doing* right now? Write it down and ask Him to help you begin to act in obedience, and eventually your feelings will follow suit as this scripture promises:

> **Roll your works upon the Lord [commit and trust them wholly to Him; He will cause your thoughts to become agreeable to His will, and] so shall your plans be established and succeed.**
>
> **— Proverbs 16:3 (*AMPC*)**

CLAIM YOUR FREE RESOURCE!

As a way of introducing you further to the teaching ministry of Rick Renner, we would like to send you FREE of charge his teaching, "How To Receive a Miraculous Touch From God" on CD or as an MP3 download.

In His earthly ministry, Jesus commonly healed *all* who were sick of *all* their diseases. In this profound message, learn about the manifold dimensions of Christ's wisdom, goodness, power, and love toward all humanity who came to Him in faith with their needs.

☑ **YES, I want to receive Rick Renner's monthly teaching letter!**

Simply scan the QR code to claim this resource or go to:
renner.org/claim-your-free-offer

WITH US!

renner.org

- facebook.com/rickrenner • facebook.com/rennerdenise
- youtube.com/rennerministries • youtube.com/deniserenner
- instagram.com/rickrrenner • instagram.com/rennerministries_
  instagram.com/rennerdenise